ROCK
CHORD
GUIDE

Harvey Vinson

PHOTOGRAPHS

Elliot Landy: Front and Back Inside Cover, Pages 25,
                27, 46, 51, 59, 62, 74, 77, 89, and 95
Jay Good: Pages 19, 23, 31, and 83
Mark Amerling: Pages 10 and 85
Richard Klein: Pages 17 and 65
Ray Flerlage: Pages 39 and 69
David Gahr: Page 49

Book design by Jean Hammons

ISBN 0-8256-2147-X
Library of Congress Catalog Number 70-85514

CONTENTS

INTRODUCTION

The chords illustrated in this book are the same ones used by professional rock guitarists—you should be familiar with all of them. The chords more frequently used by rock guitarists are marked ✳ and should be studied first. A knowledge of these chords will enable you to play most rock tunes. A complete catalogue of all the chords in this book is presented in *Appendix A.*

There is nothing more disconcerting than a guitar which is out of tune. If you are unsure of how to tune your instrument or if you want to refresh your memory, see *Appendix B* for complete and detailed tuning instructions.

Standard guitar notations are used in this book. The numbers 1—4 indicate which finger to use when making a specific chord.

These numbers appear in the chord diagrams and are designed to show you the most practical and comfortable fingerings. Every chord is clearly illustrated with photographs to help you find the proper frets and strings.

E CHORD

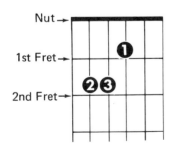

When you finger a chord with the left hand, it is very important to place the fingers as close to the frets as you can. In the E chord the 1st finger should be right behind the 1st fret. The 2nd and 3rd fingers should be right behind the 2nd fret.

SECTION ONE
chords with root (letter name) on 6th string

THE MAJOR CHORD*

We shall begin with the important E Major chord:

E MAJOR CHORD

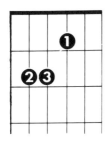

Strum this chord slowly making sure all the strings are sounding. If any of the strings sound weak or buzz, make sure you have the correct fingering with the fingertips pressing down the strings as close to the frets as is comfortable. Keep your left hand fingernails clipped short. If you're sure you have the right fingering but the chord sounds strange, your guitar is probably out of tune. *Appendix B* contains tuning instructions.

The E Major chord is very useful because it can be "barred" easily. First, substitute the alternate left hand fingering shown here.

E MAJOR CHORD

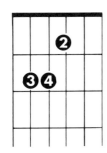

Now, slide this fingering towards you a few frets.

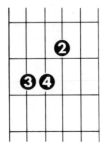

Place your left hand index finger across all six strings one fret below this fingering formation. This technique is called "barring." Play this chord using the bar at a few different frets.

MOVABLE MAJOR CHORD

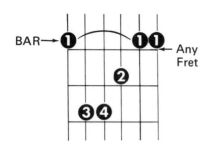

Using light-gauge strings on your guitar makes bar chords such as this much easier to play. "Guild Sidewinder" guitar strings and "Fender Rock 'n' Roll Strings" are two brand names used by professionals.

By using a bar with the E Major chord you have converted it into a movable major chord. This means you now know about fifteen major chords! To understand where to locate these major chords, examine the note chart at the right.

The letters (E, F, F#, G, etc.) stand for the notes produced by the 6th string at various frets.

Guitar strings are numbered from 1 to 6 starting with the highest sounding string (1st string) and going to the lowest sounding string (6th string). The string closest to you is the 6th string.

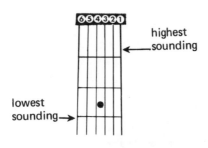

highest sounding

lowest sounding

NOTES PRODUCED
BY THE 6TH STRING

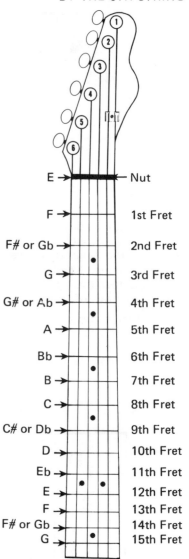

E	Nut
F	1st Fret
F# or Gb	2nd Fret
G	3rd Fret
G# or Ab	4th Fret
A	5th Fret
Bb	6th Fret
B	7th Fret
C	8th Fret
C# or Db	9th Fret
D	10th Fret
Eb	11th Fret
E	12th Fret
F	13th Fret
F# or Gb	14th Fret
G	15th Fret

The letter name of the movable major chord you know is determined by the position the bar takes on the 6th string. For example, when the bar is behind the 1st fret the 6th string produces F. Thus, you have an F Major chord.

F MAJOR CHORD

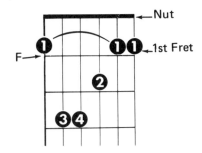

When the bar is behind the 3rd fret, the 6th string produces G. So you have a G Major chord.

G* (G MAJOR CHORD)

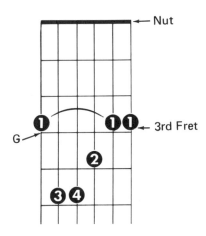

You can make this bar chord behind any fret (all the way up to the fifteenth fret!). Just remember: the letter name of the chord is determined by the position the bar takes on the 6th string.

Here's some very important theory: *the letter name of a chord is actually known as the ROOT of the chord.* So the above movable chord is called a ROOT 6 BAR CHORD. This means that the ROOT (or letter name) of the chord is found on the 6th string, and that chord is a bar chord.

The entire first section of this book deals with ROOT 6 BAR CHORDS so you can see why it is important to know the notes produced by the 6th string.

The standard abbreviation for a major chord is the letter name of the chord alone. For example, when you see just the letter "G," play a G Major chord.

To make certain you understand how and where to locate the movable major chord, play the following progression known in rock circles as the "blues progression." Count slowly and evenly from 1 to 4 playing the indicated chord on the indicated count.

BLUES PROGRESSION

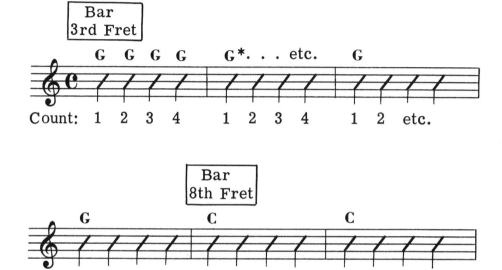

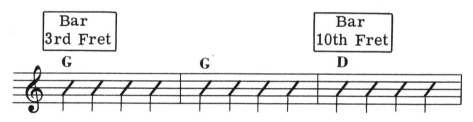

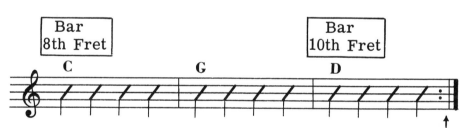

This is a repeat sign and means to repeat the entire progression from the beginning.

*With this type of music notation, continue to play the same chord until a different chord is indicated. In other words, play the G chord for the first four measures changing to a C chord in the fifth measure.

THE 6th CHORD *

By placing the 4th finger on the 2nd string, you convert the E chord into an E 6th chord:

E 6TH CHORD

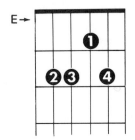 

By using the E 6th chord formation with a bar you can play over fifteen 6th chords!

MOVABLE 6TH CHORD

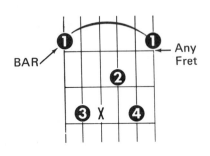 

The "X" on the 4th string means that you "damp" the sound of that string. Do this by allowing the 3rd finger to touch (but not press down) the 4th string. With the 4th string dampened, you should not hear any sound from that string when you strum this chord.

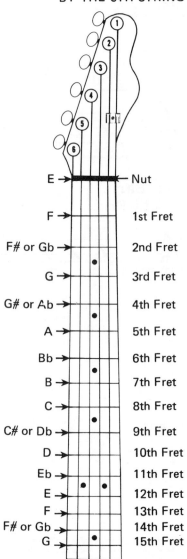

NOTES PRODUCED
BY THE 6TH STRING

E →	Nut
F →	1st Fret
F# or Gb →	2nd Fret
G →	3rd Fret
G# or Ab →	4th Fret
A →	5th Fret
Bb →	6th Fret
B →	7th Fret
C →	8th Fret
C# or Db →	9th Fret
D →	10th Fret
Eb →	11th Fret
E →	12th Fret
F →	13th Fret
F# or Gb →	14th Fret
G →	15th Fret

Because this 6th chord is a ROOT 6 BAR CHORD, the letter name of the chord is determined by the position the bar takes on the 6th string.

When the bar is behind the 1st fret, you have an F 6th chord; behind the 3rd fret you have a G 6th chord; behind the 5th fret you have an A 6th chord.

Make this bar chord behind any fret.

6th chords themselves are used rather sparingly in rock 'n' roll music. Substitute 6th chords for major chords of the same letter name when you want a slightly more interesting sound. The next example illustrates where 6th chords are used in the blues progression. After you play the major chord, simply move the 4th finger to the 2nd string to create the 6th chord. The bar with the rest of the fingers remains in the same position with both chords. This will become clearer to you as you play. Remember to dampen the 4th string when you strum the 6th chord.

BLUES IN F

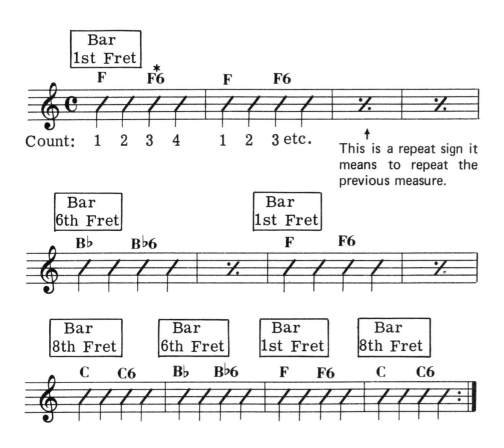

The standard abbreviation for a 6th chord is simply the number 6. F6 indicates an F 6th chord.

13

THE 7th CHORD

By placing the 4th finger on the 2nd string, you also convert the E chord into an E 7th chord:

E 7TH CHORD

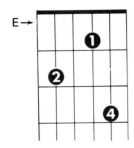

Here is the E 7th chord formation with a bar.

MOVABLE 7TH CHORD

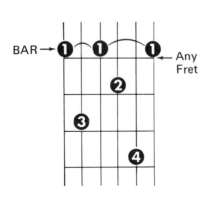

Because this 7th chord is a ROOT 6 BAR CHORD, the letter name of the chord is determined by the position the bar takes on the 6th string.

When the bar is behind the 1st fret, you have an F 7th chord; behind the 3rd fret you have a G 7th chord; behind the 5th fret you have an A 7th chord.

Make this bar chord behind any fret.

NOTES PRODUCED BY THE 6TH STRING

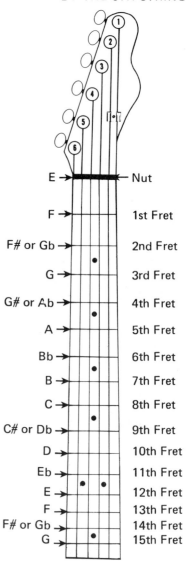

E →	Nut
F →	1st Fret
F# or Gb →	2nd Fret
G →	3rd Fret
G# or Ab →	4th Fret
A →	5th Fret
Bb →	6th Fret
B →	7th Fret
C →	8th Fret
C# or Db →	9th Fret
D →	10th Fret
Eb →	11th Fret
E →	12th Fret
F →	13th Fret
F# or Gb →	14th Fret
G →	15th Fret

The first three chords in this book (the major chord, the 6th chord, and the 7th chord) are frequently used together. The following blues illustrates this. Count slowly and evenly, "1...&...2...&...3...&...4...&...1...&...etc.," strumming once on each number and on each "&." After you can comfortably play this blues at a slow speed, try it on the fast side. Compare this blues to the other blues you've worked on.

BLUES IN F

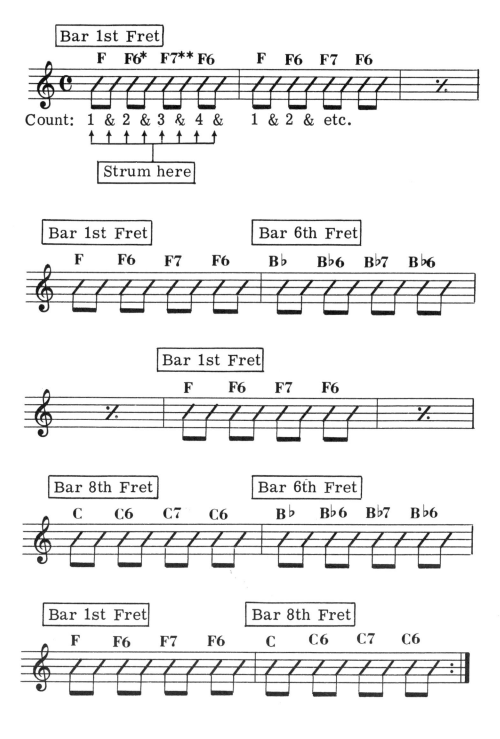

The F 6th chord becomes an F 7th chord when the 4th finger is moved up one fret. The entire flavor of this progression is created by the movement of the 4th finger.

**The standard abbreviation for a 7th chord is the number 7. F7 indicates an F 7th chord.*

THE AUGMENTED 9th CHORD *

The E7 chord can be changed into an E augmented 9th chord by covering both the 1st and 2nd strings with the 4th finger:

E AUGMENTED 9TH CHORD

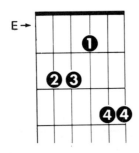

By using this chord formation with a bar, you can play any augmented 9th chord you might need.

MOVABLE AUGMENTED 9TH CHORD

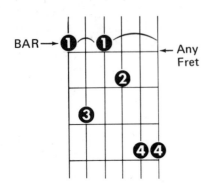

As the augmented 9th chord is a ROOT 6 BAR CHORD, the letter name of this chord is determined by the position the bar takes on the 6th string. You shouldn't have any trouble locating this chord as the fingering is very similar to the 7th chord.

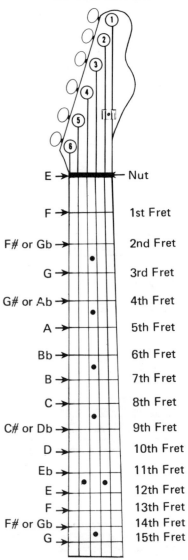

NOTES PRODUCED
BY THE 6TH STRING

E	Nut
F	1st Fret
F# or Gb	2nd Fret
G	3rd Fret
G# or Ab	4th Fret
A	5th Fret
Bb	6th Fret
B	7th Fret
C	8th Fret
C# or Db	9th Fret
D	10th Fret
Eb	11th Fret
E	12th Fret
F	13th Fret
F# or Gb	14th Fret
G	15th Fret

When the bar is behind the 1st fret, you have an F aug.* 9th chord; behind the 3rd fret you have a G aug. 9th chord; behind the 5th fret you have an A aug. 9th chord; etc.

The augmented 9th chord is frequently combined with the major chord of the same letter name to create chordal (harmonic) interest. Go through this next example playing only on the indicated counts and not on the quarter note rests ⁊ . Keep the bar behind the 2nd fret for entire example.

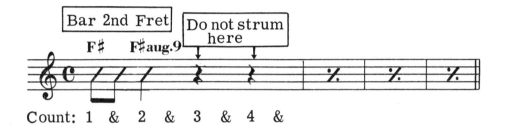

Count: 1 & 2 & 3 & 4 &

You can add interest to the progression by accenting (>) the augmented 9th chord. Go through the last example again.

*The word "augmented" is frequently abbreviated aug. or +. F aug. 9 and F+9 both indicate an F augmented 9th chord.

The 9th CHORD

By placing the 3rd finger on the 1st string, you convert the E chord into an E 9th chord.

E 9TH CHORD

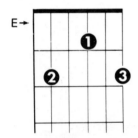

By using this chord formation with a bar, you can play over fifteen 9th chords!

MOVABLE 9TH CHORD

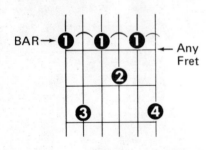

Because this 9th chord is a ROOT 6 BAR CHORD, the letter name of the chord is determined by the position the bar takes on the 6th string. Locating this chord shouldn't be a problem as the fingering is similar to the other chords we've been working with.

NOTES PRODUCED
BY THE 6TH STRING

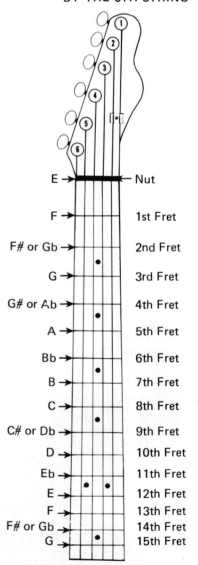

E	Nut
F	1st Fret
F# or Gb	2nd Fret
G	3rd Fret
G# or Ab	4th Fret
A	5th Fret
Bb	6th Fret
B	7th Fret
C	8th Fret
C# or Db	9th Fret
D	10th Fret
Eb	11th Fret
E	12th Fret
F	13th Fret
F# or Gb	14th Fret
G	15th Fret

18

When the bar is behind the 1st fret you have an F 9th chord; behind the 3rd fret you have a G 9th chord; behind the 5th fret an A 9th chord.

9th chords are infrequently used in rock 'n' roll music. Use a 9th chord in place of a 7th chord of the same letter name when you want a jazz-type of feeling. Play through one of the blues progressions we've worked on substituting 9th chords for 7th chords to better understand the sound of this chord.

THE MINOR CHORD *

By removing the 1st finger from the 3rd string, the E chord becomes an E minor chord:

E MINOR CHORD

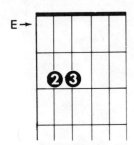

NOTES PRODUCED
BY THE 6TH STRING

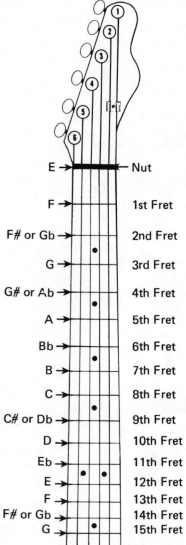

Play the E chord a few times and then the E minor chord. Listen to the difference. The minor chord has a sad, melancholy feeling that the major chord doesn't have.

MOVABLE MINOR CHORD

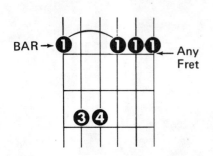

Because this minor chord is a ROOT 6 BAR CHORD, the letter name is determined by the position the bar takes on the 6th string. Locating and fingering this chord is very similar to the major chord you already know.

When the bar is behind the 1st fret you have an F minor chord; behind the 3rd fret you have a G minor chord; behind the 5th fret an A minor chord.

To give yourself a better "feel" for this chord, play the following progression using all bar chords. This progression is often called the "turn-around" and will sound quite familiar to you.

TURN-AROUND PROGRESSION

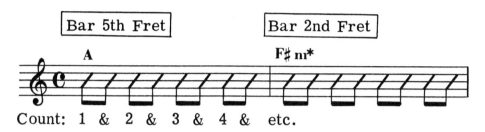

Count: 1 & 2 & 3 & 4 & etc.

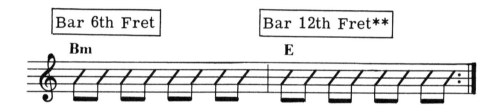

*The standard abbreviation of the minor chord is the letter name of the chord followed by a small m. F#m stands for an F# minor chord.

**If you have a difficult time barring at the 12th fret, play the E chord that doesn't use a bar (1st chord in the book).

THE MINOR 6th CHORD

By placing the 4th finger on the 2nd string, the E minor chord becomes an E minor 6th chord.

E MINOR 6TH CHORD

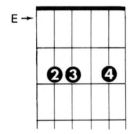

By using this chord formation with a bar, you can play over fifteen minor 6th chords!

MOVABLE MINOR 6TH CHORD

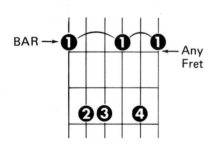

Because this minor 6th chord is a ROOT 6 BAR CHORD, the letter name is determined by the position the bar takes on the 6th string. It'll be easy to locate this chord if you'll think in terms of the minor chord you already know.

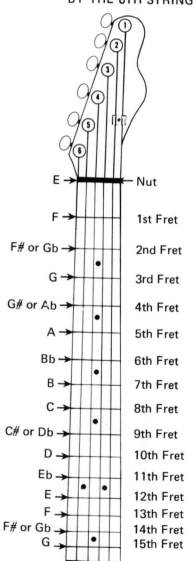

NOTES PRODUCED
BY THE 6TH STRING

E →	Nut
F →	1st Fret
F# or Gb →	2nd Fret
G →	3rd Fret
G# or Ab →	4th Fret
A →	5th Fret
Bb →	6th Fret
B →	7th Fret
C →	8th Fret
C# or Db →	9th Fret
D →	10th Fret
Eb →	11th Fret
E →	12th Fret
F →	13th Fret
F# or Gb →	14th Fret
G →	15th Fret

When the bar is behind the 1st fret you have an F minor 6th chord; behind the 3rd fret you have a G minor 6th chord; behind the 5th fret an A minor 6th chord.

The minor 6th chord is one of the more pleasant sounding chords used in rock music. You can substitute a minor 6th chord for any minor chord of the same letter name. (For example, you can substitute an Am6 chord for an Am chord.)

THE MINOR 7th CHORD*

By placing the 4th finger on the 2nd string, you also convert the E minor chord into an E minor 7th chord:

E MINOR 7TH CHORD

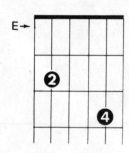 

By using this chord formation with a bar, you can play over fifteen minor 7th chords!

MOVABLE MINOR 7TH CHORD

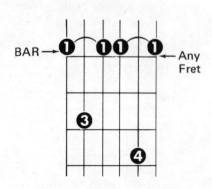 

This minor 7th chord is also a ROOT 6 BAR CHORD with the letter name of the chord being determined by the position the bar takes on the 6th string.

When the bar is behind the 1st fret you have an F minor 7th chord; behind the 3rd fret you have a G minor 7th chord; behind the 5th fret you have an A minor 7th chord; etc.

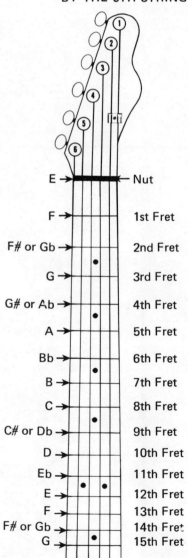

NOTES PRODUCED
BY THE 6TH STRING

E →	Nut
F →	1st Fret
F# or Gb →	2nd Fret
G →	3rd Fret
G# or Ab →	4th Fret
A →	5th Fret
Bb →	6th Fret
B →	7th Fret
C →	8th Fret
C# or Db →	9th Fret
D →	10th Fret
Eb →	11th Fret
E →	12th Fret
F →	13th Fret
F# or Gb →	14th Fret
G →	15th Fret

24

Both the minor 6th and minor 7th chords are actually variations of the minor chord of the same letter name. This will become clearer to you as you play the next progression. In the sheet music the 1st measure might have only indicated an F minor chord. Throwing in the F minor 6th and F minor 7th chords definitely improves the interest of the progression. Play it and see.

PROGRESSION

The standard abbreviation for a minor 6th chord is m6 preceded by the letter name of the chord. Fm6 stands for an F minor 6th chord. Likewise Fm7 stands for an F minor 7th chord.

THE MINOR 9th CHORD

THE MINOR 9TH CHORD

Place the 3rd finger on the 1st string and the E minor chord becomes an E minor 9th chord.

E MINOR 9TH CHORD

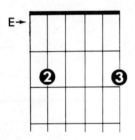

By using the E minor 9th chord formation with a bar, you can play over fifteen minor 9th chords!

MOVABLE MINOR 9TH CHORD

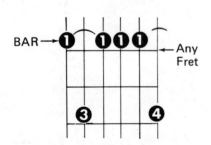

Because the minor 9th chord is a ROOT 6 BAR CHORD, the letter name of the chord is determined by the position the bar takes on the 6th string.

When the bar is behind the 1st fret, you have an F minor 9th chord; behind the 3rd fret you have a G minor 9th chord; behind the 5th fret you have an A minor 9th chord.

NOTES PRODUCED BY THE 6TH STRING

E →	← Nut
F →	1st Fret
F# or Gb →	2nd Fret
G →	3rd Fret
G# or Ab →	4th Fret
A →	5th Fret
Bb →	6th Fret
B →	7th Fret
C →	8th Fret
C# or Db →	9th Fret
D →	10th Fret
Eb →	11th Fret
E →	12th Fret
F →	13th Fret
F# or Gb →	14th Fret
G →	15th Fret

Make this bar chord behind any fret.

Minor 9th chords are used rather sparingly in rock 'n' roll music. Substitute minor 9th chords for minor chords of the same letter name when you want to create a "jazzy" feeling in a song.

THE DIMINISHED CHORD

Popularized by the early "ragtime" guitarists, the diminished chord has a very different sound from the other chords in the book. It is sometimes called the diminished 7th chord and is abbreviated *dim* or *dim 7*. (Sometimes this chord is abbreviated by "o" or "o 7.") Play this example.

E DIMINISHED CHORD

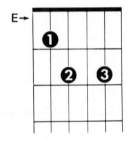

By using the E diminished chord formation with a bar, you can play over fifteen diminished chords!

MOVABLE DIMINISHED CHORD

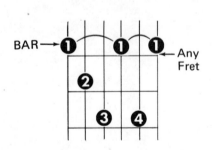

Because this diminished chord is a ROOT 6 BAR CHORD, the letter name of the chord is determined by the position the bar takes on the 6th string. When the bar is behind the 1st fret, you have an F *dim* chord; behind the 3rd fret you have a G *dim* chord; behind the 5th fret you have an

Make this bar chord behind any fret.

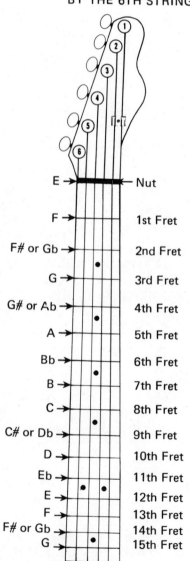

NOTES PRODUCED
BY THE 6TH STRING

E →	← Nut
F →	1st Fret
F# or Gb →	2nd Fret
G →	3rd Fret
G# or Ab →	4th Fret
A →	5th Fret
Bb →	6th Fret
B →	7th Fret
C →	8th Fret
C# or Db →	9th Fret
D →	10th Fret
Eb →	11th Fret
E →	12th Fret
F →	13th Fret
F# or Gb →	14th Fret
G →	15th Fret

To better understand where the diminished chord is generally used, play this next short progression. Notice that the diminished chord is used in the introduction and the ending of the song.

SHORT PROGRESSION

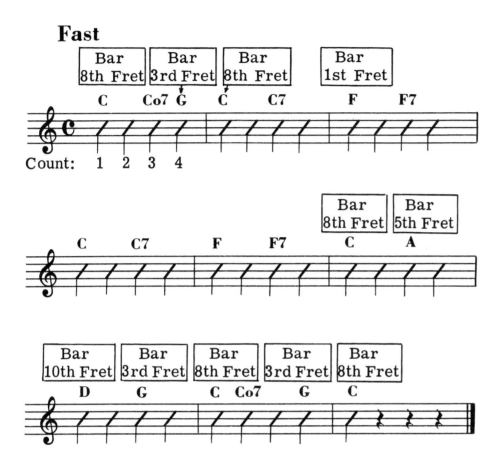

THE MAJOR CHORD

Here's a somewhat different formation of a ROOT 6 major chord:

G MAJOR CHORD

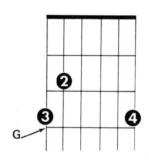

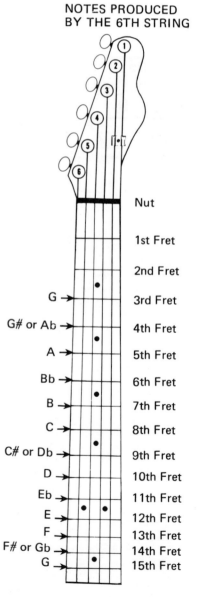

NOTES PRODUCED
BY THE 6TH STRING

Nut

1st Fret

2nd Fret

G →   3rd Fret

G# or Ab →   4th Fret

A →   5th Fret

Bb →   6th Fret

B →   7th Fret

C →   8th Fret

C# or Db →   9th Fret

D →   10th Fret

Eb →   11th Fret

E →   12th Fret

F →   13th Fret

F# or Gb →   14th Fret

G →   15th Fret

By using the G chord formation with a bar, you can play an entirely new set of major chords. Although this formation of the major chord is not as popular as the preceding one, many situations arise where this formation is quite useful. Carefully note that the bar *does not include* the 5th and 6th strings. When the bar excludes these two strings the chord is much easier to form.

MOVABLE MAJOR CHORD

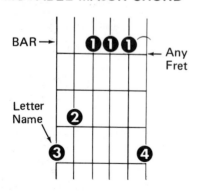

Unlike the other ROOT 6 major chord, the letter name of the major chord is determined by the position of the 3rd finger on the 6th string. When the 3rd finger is behind the 5th fret you have an A chord; behind the 7th fret you have a B chord; behind the 8th fret you have a C chord; etc.

Make this bar chord behind any fret.

Play this next popular progression to familiarize yourself with this new chord. Note that although the A chord calls for a bar at the 2nd fret, the 3rd finger is on the 6th string behind the 5th fret.

POPULAR PROGRESSION

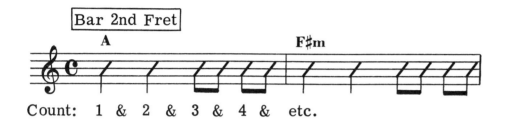

Count: 1 & 2 & 3 & 4 & etc.

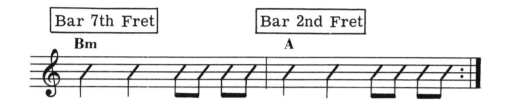

THE 6th CHORD

By removing the 4th finger from the 1st string, you convert the G chord you just learned into a G 6th chord!

G 6TH CHORD

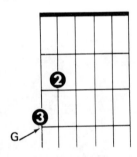

By using this chord formation with a bar, you learn a whole new set of 6th chords.

MOVABLE 6TH CHORD

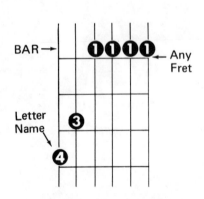

As this 6th chord is a ROOT 6 BAR CHORD, the letter name of the chord is determined by the position of the 4th finger on the 6th string.

When the 4th finger is behind the 5th fret, you have an A 6th chord; behind the 7th fret you have a B 6th chord; behind the 8th fret you have a C 6th chord.

Although you'll only find occasional use for this chord, every chord you learn adds to your capabilities as a musician.

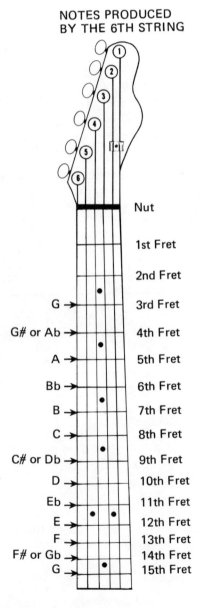

NOTES PRODUCED BY THE 6TH STRING

	Nut
	1st Fret
	2nd Fret
G →	3rd Fret
G# or Ab →	4th Fret
A →	5th Fret
Bb →	6th Fret
B →	7th Fret
C →	8th Fret
C# or Db →	9th Fret
D →	10th Fret
Eb →	11th Fret
E →	12th Fret
F →	13th Fret
F# or Gb →	14th Fret
G →	15th Fret

THE 7th CHORD

By placing the 1st finger on the 1st string, you convert the G chord we've been working on into a G 7th chord:

G 7TH CHORD

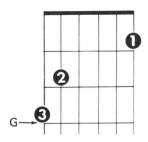

You'll have to stretch your left hand fingers a bit to finger the 7th chord with a bar.

MOVABLE 7TH CHORD

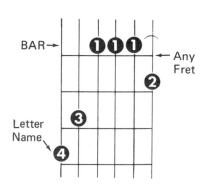

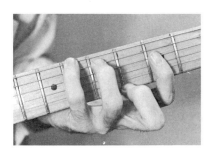

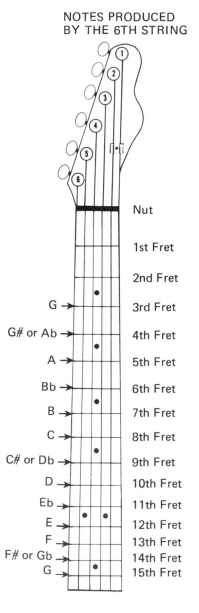

	Nut
	1st Fret
	2nd Fret
G →	3rd Fret
G# or Ab →	4th Fret
A →	5th Fret
Bb →	6th Fret
B →	7th Fret
C →	8th Fret
C# or Db →	9th Fret
D →	10th Fret
Eb →	11th Fret
E →	12th Fret
F →	13th Fret
F# or Gb →	14th Fret
G →	15th Fret

As this 7th chord is a ROOT 6 BAR CHORD, the letter name of the chord is determined by the position of the 4th finger on the 6th string.

When the 4th finger is behind the 5th fret, you have an A 7th chord; behind the 7th fret you have a B 7th chord; behind the 8th fret you have a C 7th chord.

Make this bar chord behind any fret.

THE MAJOR 7th CHORD

The ROOT 6 major 7th chord can only be played as a movable chord. Notice that both the 1st and 5th strings are "dampened" by the 1st finger of the left hand. This technique is a little tricky so you'll have to spend some time on it. The quality of the major 7th chord is completely lost if either of these two strings are allowed to sound. Play this chord from the 2nd fret up to the 15th.

MOVABLE MAJOR 7TH CHORD

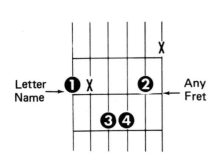

As this major 7th chord is a ROOT 6 CHORD, the letter name of the chord is determined by the position of the 1st finger on the 6th string.

When the 1st finger is behind the 3rd fret, you have a G Maj. 7th chord ("Maj." is an abbreviation for major); behind the 5th fret you have an A Maj. 7th chord; behind the 8th fret a C Maj. 7th chord; etc.

In rock music, the major 7th chord is often used as the last chord in a piece. For example, if you are playing a song in the key of A you might end the song with an A Maj. 7th chord.

Make this major 7th chord behind any fret.

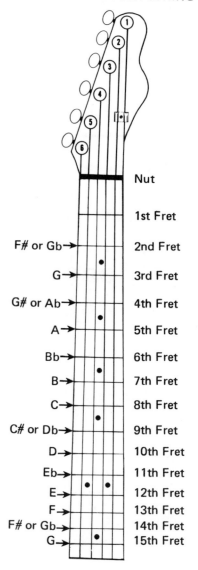

NOTES PRODUCED BY THE 6TH STRING

	Nut
	1st Fret
F# or Gb →	2nd Fret
G →	3rd Fret
G# or Ab →	4th Fret
A →	5th Fret
Bb →	6th Fret
B →	7th Fret
C →	8th Fret
C# or Db →	9th Fret
D →	10th Fret
Eb →	11th Fret
E →	12th Fret
F →	13th Fret
F# or Gb →	14th Fret
G →	15th Fret

THE EXERCISE USING ROOT 6 BAR CHORDS

This exercise puts to practical use every chord you have learned so far. Although the following progression does not belong to any particular song, you will find it a useful way to remember the names of the chords you've learned. The exercise is also designed to strengthen the muscles of your left hand.

EXERCISE

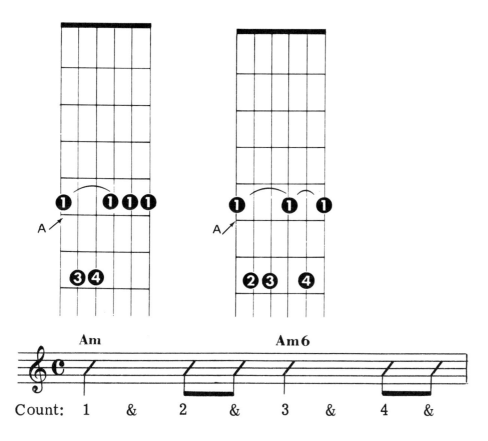

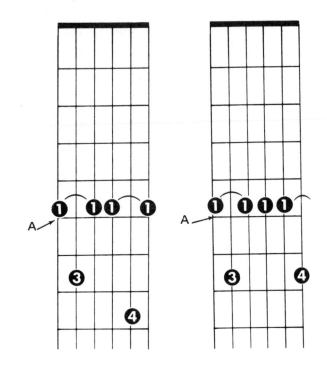

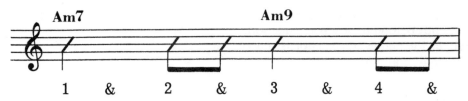

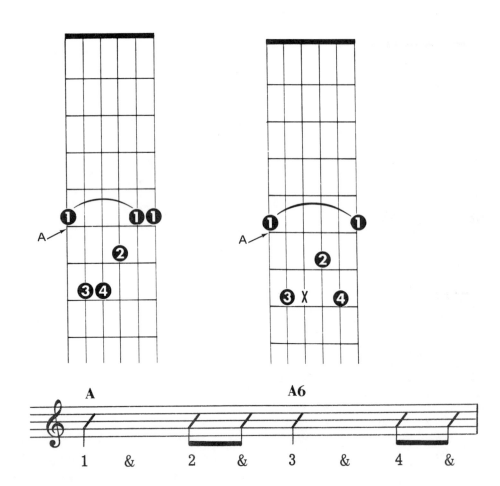

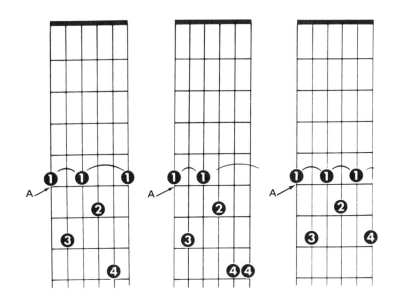

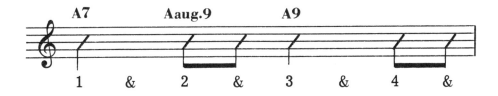

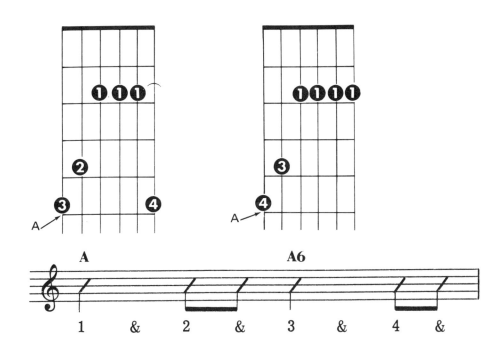

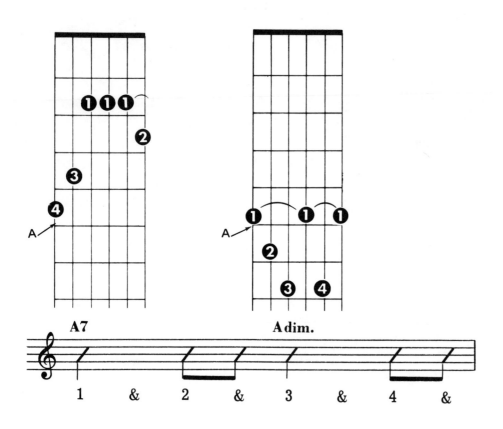

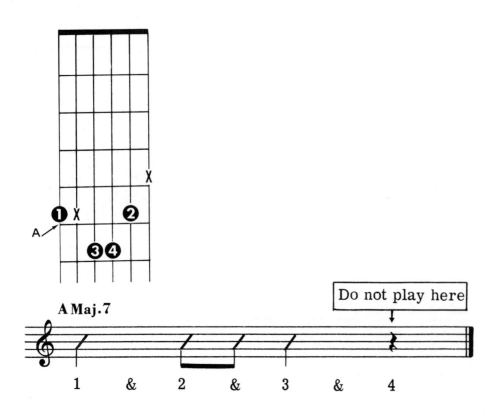

An excellent idea is to play this progression in a few other keys. Say the name of the chord out loud as you play it. By moving the progression up one fret you can play the exercise in Bb.

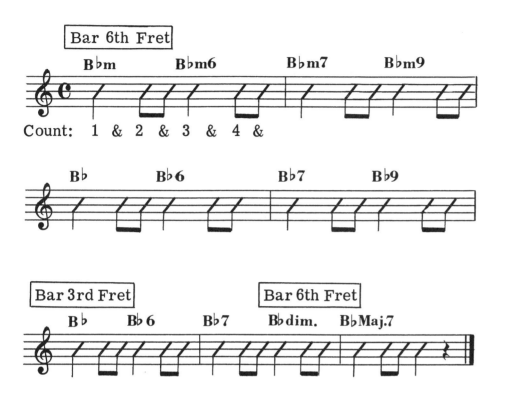

SECTION TWO
chords with root (letter name) on 5th string

Now we'll concern ourselves with an important series of chords that have their root on the 5th string: the ROOT 5 BAR CHORDS. All you need to know to play the ROOT 5 BAR CHORDS are the chord formations plus the notes produced by the 5th string.

Examine the note chart at the right:

The letters (A, Bb, B, C, etc.) stand for the notes produced by the 5th string at various frets. For example, the 5th string "open" (unfingered) produces the note A; when you push down behind the 1st fret the 5th string produces Bb; behind the 3rd fret the 5th string produces C; etc. Go up and down the 5th string a few times playing and saying out loud the note each fret produces. After you're familiar with these notes (don't try to memorize them now), start working on the next important rock chord: the major chord.

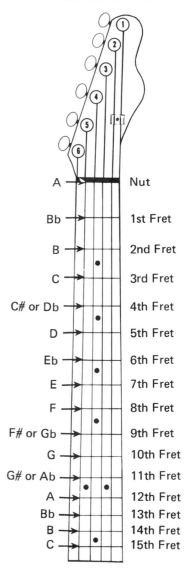

NOTES PRODUCED
BY THE 5TH STRING

A	Nut
Bb	1st Fret
B	2nd Fret
C	3rd Fret
C# or Db	4th Fret
D	5th Fret
Eb	6th Fret
E	7th Fret
F	8th Fret
F# or Gb	9th Fret
G	10th Fret
G# or Ab	11th Fret
A	12th Fret
Bb	13th Fret
B	14th Fret
C	15th Fret

THE MAJOR CHORD ✳

Examine and play this first ROOT 5 CHORD!

A CHORD

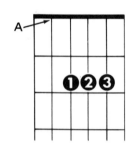

As this major chord uses the open 5th string as its root, when you use the A chord formation with a bar you have a movable major chord.

MOVABLE MAJOR CHORD

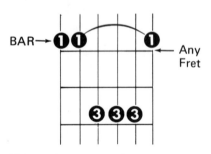

If you have trouble barring three strings with the 3rd finger, try using light-gauge strings. Be careful not to allow the 3rd finger to touch the 1st string. Spend some time practicing this chord formation as it is an extremely useful one.

As this major chord is a ROOT 5 BAR CHORD, the letter name of the chord is determined by the position the bar takes on the 5th string.

When the bar is behind the 1st fret, you have a Bb Major chord; behind the 3rd fret you have a C Major chord; behind the 5th fret you have a D Major chord.

Make this bar chord behind any fret.

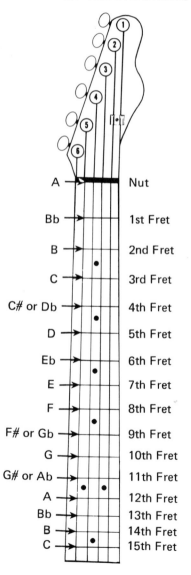

NOTES PRODUCED
BY THE 5TH STRING

A	Nut
Bb	1st Fret
B	2nd Fret
C	3rd Fret
C# or Db	4th Fret
D	5th Fret
Eb	6th Fret
E	7th Fret
F	8th Fret
F# or Gb	9th Fret
G	10th Fret
G# or Ab	11th Fret
A	12th Fret
Bb	13th Fret
B	14th Fret
C	15th Fret

One of the greatest advantages of the ROOT 5 BAR CHORD is the ease with which you can switch from one chord to the next. If you're playing a progression where you have a G chord going to a C chord—play the G chord with a ROOT 6 BAR CHORD and then, without lifting the bar, play the C chord with a ROOT 5 BAR CHORD. The following exercise makes this clearer.

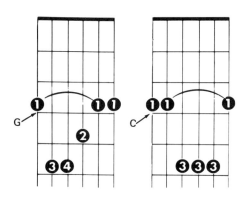

When you play, try to use chords that are physically close to each other. The chord progression usually sounds better and the chords themselves are easier to finger.

THE 6th CHORD ✳

By placing the 4th finger on the 1st string, you convert the A chord into an A 6th chord (optional fingering). An easier fingering is to bar the first four strings with the 1st finger.

A 6TH CHORD

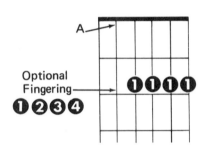

By using this chord formation with a bar you can play over fifteen 6th chords! Try a few.

MOVABLE 6TH CHORD

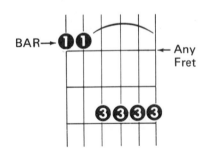

As this 6th chord is a ROOT 5 BAR CHORD, the letter name of the chord is determined by the position the bar takes on the 5th string.

When the bar is behind the 1st fret, you have a Bb 6th chord; behind the 3rd fret you have a C 6th chord; behind the 5th fret you have a D 6th chord.

Make this bar chord behind any fret.

NOTES PRODUCED BY THE 5TH STRING

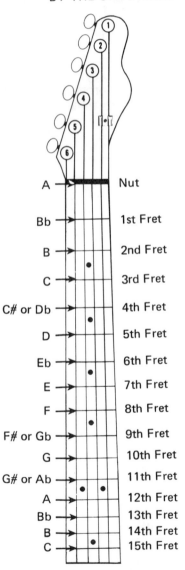

A	Nut
Bb	1st Fret
B	2nd Fret
C	3rd Fret
C# or Db	4th Fret
D	5th Fret
Eb	6th Fret
E	7th Fret
F	8th Fret
F# or Gb	9th Fret
G	10th Fret
G# or Ab	11th Fret
A	12th Fret
Bb	13th Fret
B	14th Fret
C	15th Fret

THE 7th CHORD ✳

The 4th finger on the 1st string also converts the A chord into an A 7th chord (optional fingering). As before, try barring with the 1st finger for an easier fingering.

A 7TH CHORD

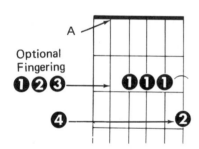

Try this chord with a bar.

MOVABLE 7TH CHORD

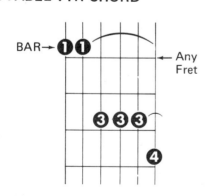

As this 7th chord is a ROOT 5 BAR CHORD, the letter name of the chord is determined by the position the bar takes on the 5th string.

When the bar is behind the 1st fret, you have a Bb 7th chord; behind the 3rd fret you have a C 7th chord; behind the 5th fret you have a D 7th chord.

Make this bar chord behind any fret.

NOTES PRODUCED BY THE 5TH STRING

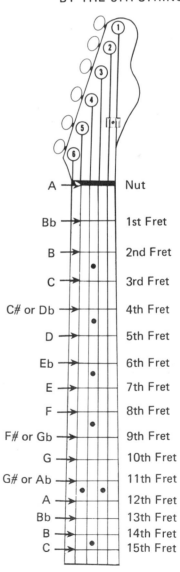

A	Nut
Bb	1st Fret
B	2nd Fret
C	3rd Fret
C# or Db	4th Fret
D	5th Fret
Eb	6th Fret
E	7th Fret
F	8th Fret
F# or Gb	9th Fret
G	10th Fret
G# or Ab	11th Fret
A	12th Fret
Bb	13th Fret
B	14th Fret
C	15th Fret

The first three chords presented in this section are frequently used together. In the next example, keep the bar behind the 3rd fret for all three chords.

EXERCISE

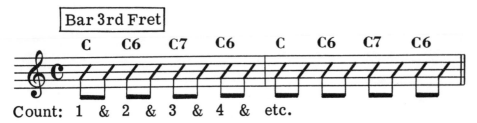

Play the last exercise at the 5th fret (D, D6, D7, etc.) and at the 7th fret (E, E6, E7, etc.). This is a very important chord progression in rock music, and you should be able to play it with ease.

Often the ROOT 6 BAR CHORDS and the ROOT 5 BAR CHORDS are used together to play the blues progression. It is very important to master this next progression to better understand how these two bar chords are used together. Notice that you keep the bar behind the 3rd fret for most of the progression.

BLUES PROGRESSION

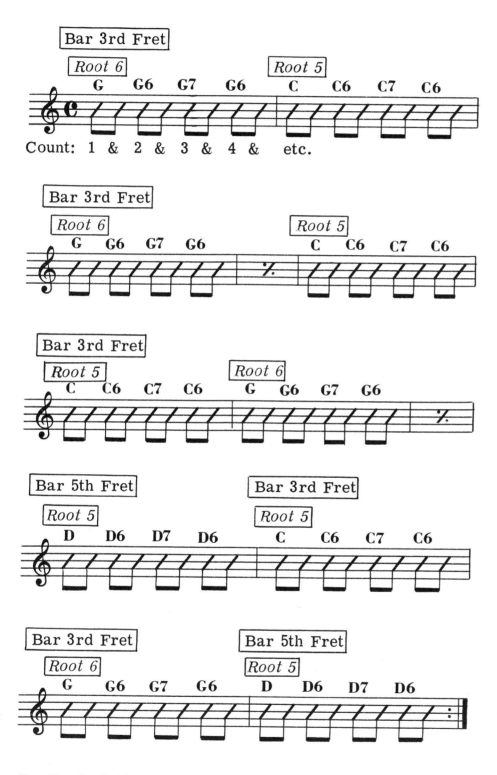

The "key" of this blues is said to be G because the first chord is G. If somebody says, "Let's play a blues in G," play the blues progression illustrated. For a Blues in A, move the entire progression up two frets so that the first chord (ROOT 6 BAR CHORD) is an A chord. For a blues in B, start the progression at the 7th fret (ROOT 6 B chord).

THE MAJOR 7th CHORD

By rearranging the 1st and 2nd finger of the left hand, the A chord becomes an A Maj. 7th chord:

A MAJOR 7TH CHORD

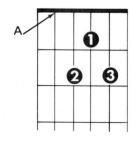

Try this chord with a bar.

MOVABLE MAJOR 7TH CHORD

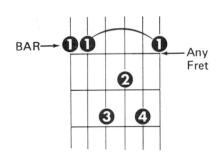

As this major 7th chord is a ROOT 5 BAR CHORD, the letter name of the chord is determined by the position the bar takes on the 5th string. Locate this chord the same way you locate the ROOT 5 major chord.

When the bar is behind the 1st fret, you have a Bb Maj. 7th chord; behind the 3rd fret you have a C Maj. 7th chord; behind the 5th fret a D Maj. 7th chord; etc.

The major 7th chord is often used as the last chord in a rock song.

NOTES PRODUCED BY THE 5TH STRING

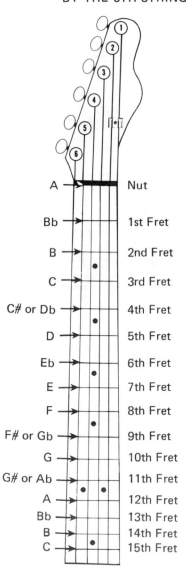

A	Nut
Bb	1st Fret
B	2nd Fret
C	3rd Fret
C# or Db	4th Fret
D	5th Fret
Eb	6th Fret
E	7th Fret
F	8th Fret
F# or Gb	9th Fret
G	10th Fret
G# or Ab	11th Fret
A	12th Fret
Bb	13th Fret
B	14th Fret
C	15th Fret

THE MINOR CHORD *

The ROOT 5 minor chord is an important and useful rock chord. Finger and play the "open" A minor chord.

A MINOR CHORD

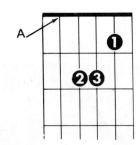

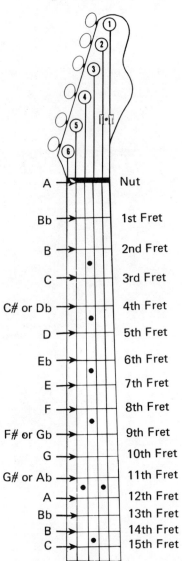

NOTES PRODUCED
BY THE 5TH STRING

A →	Nut
Bb →	1st Fret
B →	2nd Fret
C →	3rd Fret
C# or Db →	4th Fret
D →	5th Fret
Eb →	6th Fret
E →	7th Fret
F →	8th Fret
F# or Gb →	9th Fret
G →	10th Fret
G# or Ab →	11th Fret
A →	12th Fret
Bb →	13th Fret
B →	14th Fret
C →	15th Fret

Used with a bar, this minor chord formation adds about fifteen additional minor chords to your vocabulary.

MOVABLE MINOR CHORD

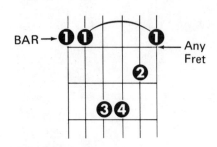

As this minor chord is a ROOT 5 BAR CHORD, the letter name of the chord is determined by the position the bar takes on the 5th string.

When the bar is behind the 1st fret, you have a Bb minor chord; behind the 3rd fret you have a C minor chord; behind the 5th fret you have a D minor chord.

Make this bar chord behind any fret.

To help you understand where to use this chord, play the next progression.
The *turn-around progression* is usually played on the slow side.

TURN-AROUND PROGRESSION

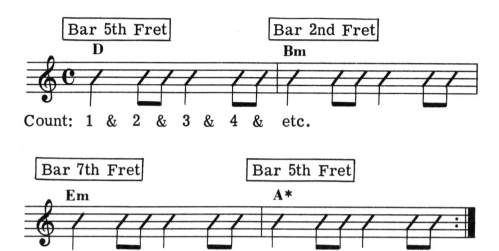

Count: 1 & 2 & 3 & 4 & etc.

An A chord at the 5th fret could only be a ROOT 6 BAR CHORD. The fret number indicates whether a ROOT 5 or ROOT 6 BAR CHORD is to be used.

THE MINOR 6th CHORD

The 4th finger on the 1st string converts the A minor chord into an A minor 6th chord:

A MINOR 6TH CHORD

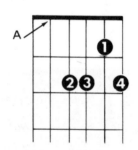 

Using the A minor 6th chord formation with a bar, you can play an entire new series of minor 6th chords.

MOVABLE MINOR 6TH CHORD

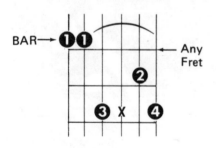 

The "X" on the 3rd string indicates that the finger blocks the sound from that string.

As this minor 6th chord is a ROOT 5 BAR CHORD, the letter name of the chord is determined by the position the bar takes on the 5th string. As this chord is similar in construction to the ROOT 5 minor chord, locating it should present no new problems.

When the bar is behind the 1st fret, you have a Bb minor 6th chord; behind the 3rd fret you have a C minor 6th chord; behind the 5th fret you have a D minor 6th chord.

Make this bar chord behind any fret.

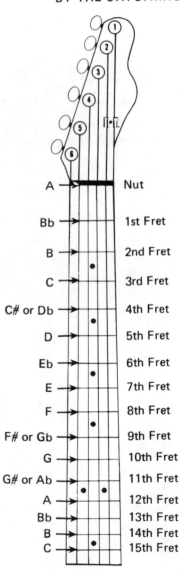

NOTES PRODUCED
BY THE 5TH STRING

A	Nut
Bb	1st Fret
B	2nd Fret
C	3rd Fret
C# or Db	4th Fret
D	5th Fret
Eb	6th Fret
E	7th Fret
F	8th Fret
F# or Gb	9th Fret
G	10th Fret
G# or Ab	11th Fret
A	12th Fret
Bb	13th Fret
B	14th Fret
C	15th Fret

THE MINOR 7th CHORD*

The 4th finger on the 1st string also converts the A minor chord into the important A minor 7th chord:

A MINOR 7TH CHORD

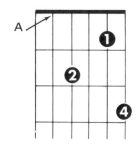

Try this new chord formation with a bar at a few different frets.

MOVABLE MINOR 7TH CHORD

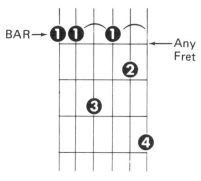

As this minor 7th chord is a ROOT 5 BAR CHORD, the letter name of the chord is determined by the position the bar takes on the 5th string. Very similar in construction to the ROOT 5 minor 6th and minor chords, its location will present no new problems.

When the bar is behind the 1st fret, you have a Bb minor 7th chord; behind the 3rd fret you have a C minor 7th chord; behind the 5th fret you have a D minor 7th chord.

Make this bar chord behind any fret.

NOTES PRODUCED BY THE 5TH STRING

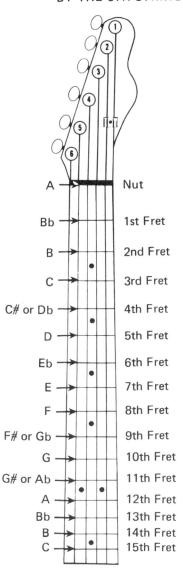

Note	Fret
A	Nut
Bb	1st Fret
B	2nd Fret
C	3rd Fret
C# or Db	4th Fret
D	5th Fret
Eb	6th Fret
E	7th Fret
F	8th Fret
F# or Gb	9th Fret
G	10th Fret
G# or Ab	11th Fret
A	12th Fret
Bb	13th Fret
B	14th Fret
C	15th Fret

The following examples illustrate where you might use the minor 6th and 7th chords. Say you're playing a song with this type of chord progression called for.

EXAMPLE #1

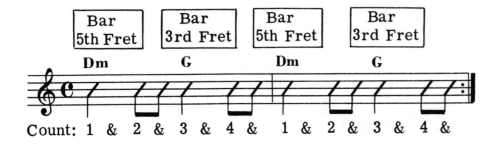

A welcomed variation is to make the second D minor chord a minor 7th chord.

EXAMPLE #2

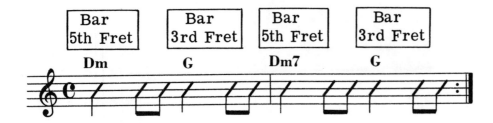

By introducing the minor 6th chord, you add even more variation.

EXAMPLE #3

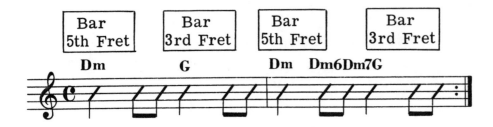

Of course you must remember not to make the variations detract from the "feel" of the song, but rather compliment it.

THE DIMINISHED CHORD

The ROOT 5 diminished chord can only be played effectively as a movable chord. If you'll compare the ROOT 6 diminished chord on page 28 with the ROOT 5 diminished chord, you'll find that they are identical. The fact is that any note in a diminished chord may serve as the root of the chord. Finger and play the movable diminished chord at a few different frets.

MOVABLE DIMINISHED CHORD

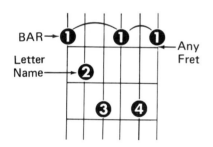

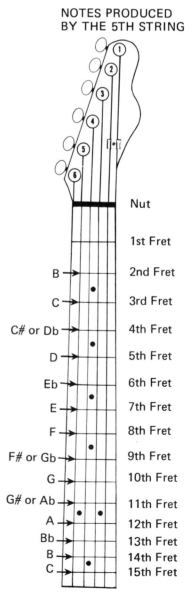

NOTES PRODUCED
BY THE 5TH STRING

Because this diminished chord is a ROOT 5 BAR CHORD, the letter name of the chord is determined by the position the *2nd finger* takes on the 5th string (thus, the letter name of the chord is *one fret higher* than the actual bar).

When the bar is behind the 1st fret, you have a B diminished chord; behind the 3rd fret you have a C# diminished chord; behind the 6th fret you have an E diminished chord.

Make this bar chord behind any fret.

THE MAJOR CHORD

Here's a somewhat different formation of a ROOT 5 major chord:

C MAJOR CHORD

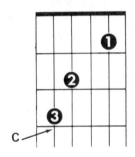

Finger and play this bar chord at a few different frets.

MOVABLE MAJOR CHORD

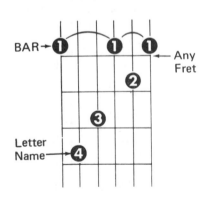

Unlike the other ROOT 5 major chord, the letter name of this major chord is determined by the position of the 4th finger on the 5th string.

When the 4th finger is behind the 5th fret, you have a D chord; behind the 7th fret you have an E chord; behind the 8th fret an F chord; etc.

Make this bar chord behind any fret.

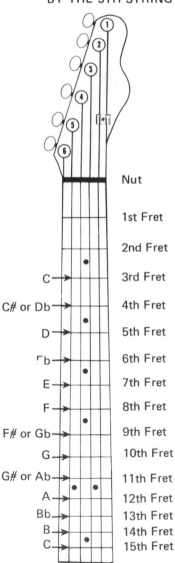

NOTES PRODUCED
BY THE 5TH STRING

Play the next progression to better understand how this new chord functions with other ROOT 5 and ROOT 6 BAR CHORDS. The progression also illustrates a slight variation of the *turn-around progression.*

TURN-AROUND PROGRESSION

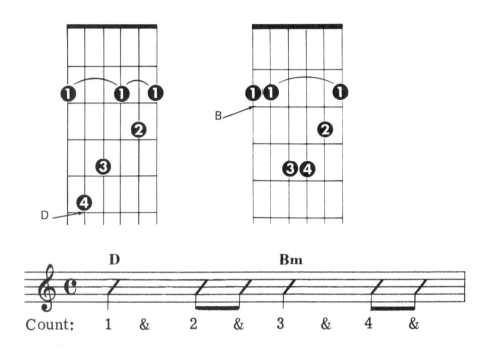

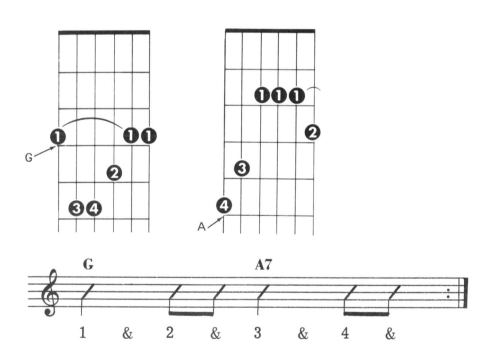

Notice that the bar remains behind the 2nd fret for the entire progression except for the G chord. Try to keep all chords in a song physically close to each other. If you can make several chords with the same bar, keep the bar in place. Try not to go jumping all over the fingerboard—many songs can be played within a three-fret area.

THE MAJOR 7th CHORD

By removing the 1st finger, the C chord you just learned becomes a C Maj. 7th chord:

C MAJOR 7TH CHORD

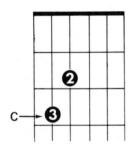

By using this chord formation with a bar, you can play over fifteen additional major 7th chords! Although this fingering of the major 7th chord is not as popular as some of the others we've worked on, every competent guitarist knows it.

MOVABLE MAJOR 7TH CHORD

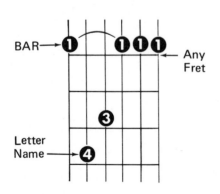

Unlike the other ROOT 5 major 7th chord, the letter name of this major 7th chord is determined by the position of the 4th finger on the 5th string.

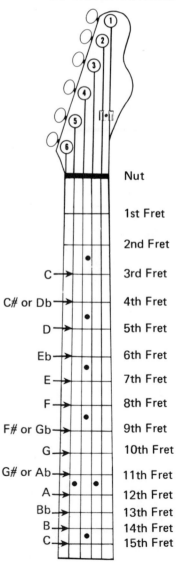

NOTES PRODUCED
BY THE 5TH STRING

Nut

1st Fret

2nd Fret

C → 3rd Fret

C# or Db → 4th Fret

D → 5th Fret

Eb → 6th Fret

E → 7th Fret

F → 8th Fret

F# or Gb → 9th Fret

G → 10th Fret

G# or Ab → 11th Fret

A → 12th Fret

Bb → 13th Fret

B → 14th Fret

C → 15th Fret

When the 4th finger is behind the 5th fret, you have a D Major 7th chord; behind the 7th fret you have an E Major 7th chord; behind the 8th fret you have an F Major 7th chord.

Make this bar chord behind any fret.

THE 7th CHORD *

By placing the 4th finger on the 3rd string, the C chord becomes the important C 7th chord.

C 7TH CHORD

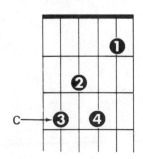

Keeping the identical fingering, the C7th chord formation becomes a movable 7th chord. Note in the diagram of the movable 7th chord that both the 1st and the 6th string are "dampened" (indicated by an "X"). Wrap the thrush of the left hand around the neck and allow it to touch the edge of the 6th string (take care not to push the string down) and dampen it. Allow the 1st finger to touch (dampen) the 1st string. Also note that there is a broken line on the 6th string. When a string is shown as a broken line, *avoid playing that string when you strum the chord.* Play this movable 7th chord many times at different frets.

MOVABLE 7TH CHORD

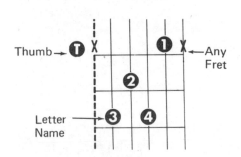

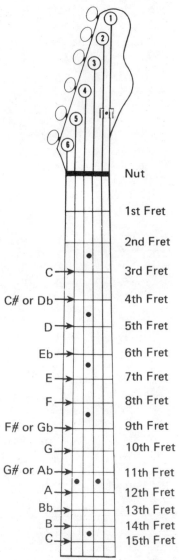

NOTES PRODUCED
BY THE 5TH STRING

	Nut
	1st Fret
	2nd Fret
C →	3rd Fret
C# or Db →	4th Fret
D →	5th Fret
Eb →	6th Fret
E →	7th Fret
F →	8th Fret
F# or Gb →	9th Fret
G →	10th Fret
G# or Ab →	11th Fret
A →	12th Fret
Bb →	13th Fret
B →	14th Fret
C →	15th Fret

Like the movable C chord and C Maj. 7th chord we've been working on, the letter name of this movable 7th chord is determined by the position of the 3rd finger on the 5th string.

When the 3rd finger is behind the 5th fret you have a D 7th chord; behind the 7th fret you have an E 7th chord; behind the 8th fret an F 7th chord; etc.

Make this chord behind any fret.

This new 7th chord is frequently used as the last chord in the blues progression. The reason for this is that your left hand stays in the same position for the second to last chord, the last chord, and the first chord in the progression. This will become clearer to you as you play this next progression.

BLUES IN G

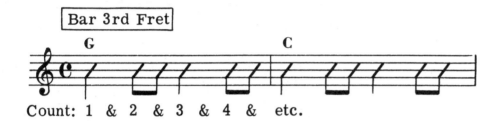

Count: 1 & 2 & 3 & 4 & etc.

Notice that when you switch from the D7 chord to the G chord, it's rather awkward to shift back to a bar chord. Many of the more skillful rock guitarists use the thumb in forming the ROOT 6 major chord at this point.

MOVABLE MAJOR CHORD (ROOT 6)

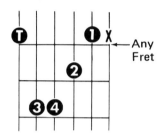

Play this chord at a few different frets to get a "feel" for it. Notice that the 1st string is dampened (as with our new 7th chord); but the thumb actually pushes down the 6th string. As this is a ROOT 6 major chord, the letter name of the chord is determined by the position the thumb takes on the 6th string. The construction of this chord is very similar to the first major chord we studied so locating it should be quite simple for you.

Here's an example of how these two chords are used together.

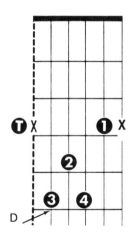
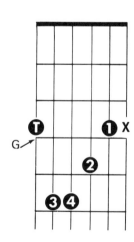

The 9th CHORD *

The ROOT 5 9th chord can only be played effectively as a movable chord. As with the two previous chords, the 6th string is dampened by the thumb of the left hand. The 6th string is indicated by a broken line which means that you should avoid playing that string when you strum the chord. (The string is dampened in case you play it by mistake.) You also bar the first three strings with the 3rd finger.

MOVABLE 9TH CHORD

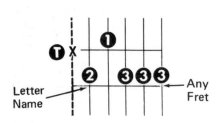

Play this chord at a few different frets to see if you can manage it. Some guitarists prefer this alternate fingering:

MOVABLE 9TH CHORD

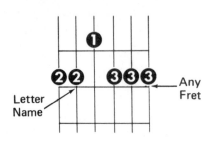

With the alternate fingering you must bar not only with the 3rd finger, but with the 2nd finger as well. The advantage is that you can play all six strings when you strum the chord.

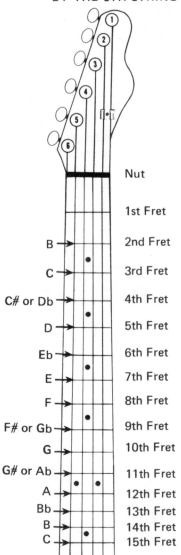

NOTES PRODUCED BY THE 5TH STRING

	Nut
	1st Fret
B	2nd Fret
C	3rd Fret
C# or Db	4th Fret
D	5th Fret
Eb	6th Fret
E	7th Fret
F	8th Fret
F# or Gb	9th Fret
G	10th Fret
G# or Ab	11th Fret
A	12th Fret
Bb	13th Fret
B	14th Fret
C	15th Fret

As both these 9th chords are ROOT 5 CHORDS, their letter names are determined by the position the 2nd finger takes on the 5th string.

When the 2nd finger is behind the 5th fret, you have a D 9th chord; behind the 7th fret you have an E 9th chord; behind the 8th fret an F 9th chord.

9th chords can be used in place of 7th chords when you want a more interesting sound.

Use either 9th chord behind any fret.

THE EXERCISE USING
ROOT 5 BAR CHORDS

The following exercise makes use of all the ROOT 5 CHORDS presented in this book. Practice this exercise until you can play it with ease. Try naming the chords out loud as you play them. Then the exercise will not only strengthen the muscles in your left hand, but add to your ability to recall these important rock chords.

EXERCISE

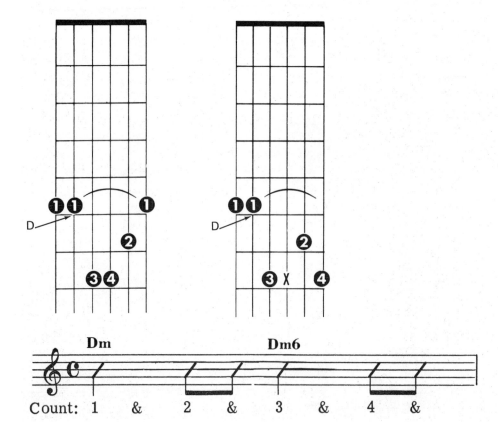

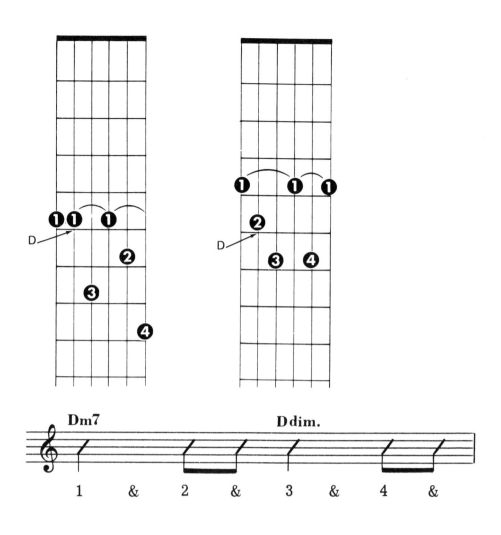

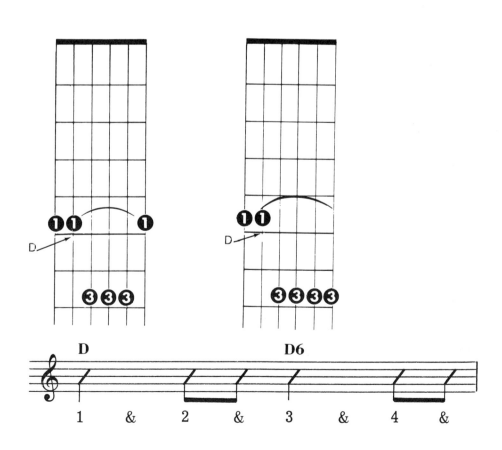

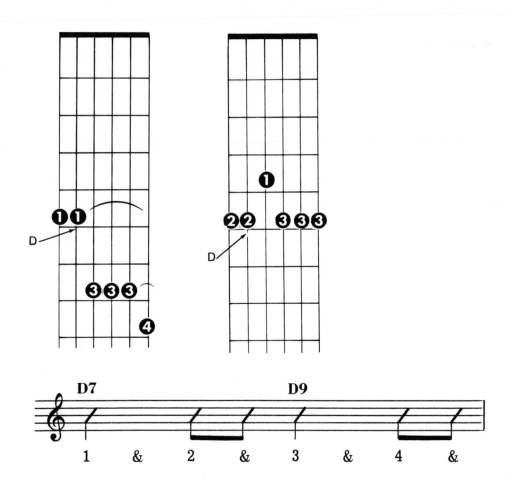

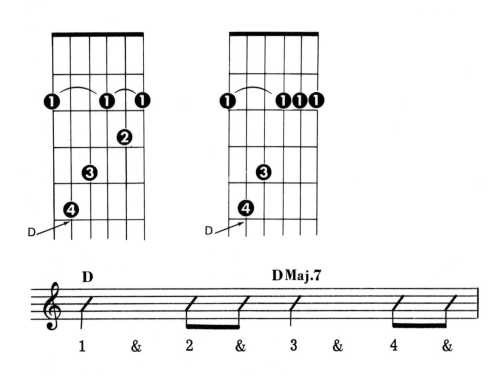

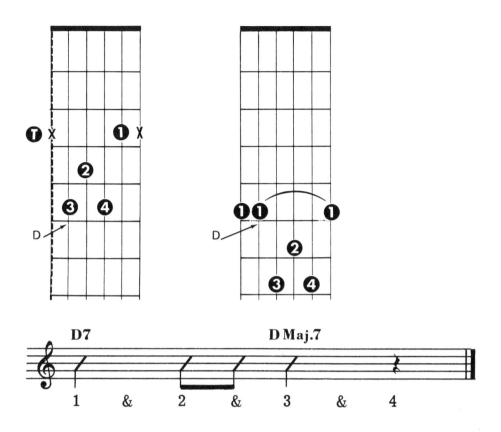

D7   **D Maj.7**

1 & 2 & 3 & 4

Play this chord progression in a few other keys (starting at the 6th or 7th fret) following the same procedure outlined above.

SECTION THREE
chords with root (letter name) on 4th string

This last series of chords have their root on the 4th string: the ROOT 4 BAR CHORDS. One of the main differences between the ROOT 4 BAR CHORDS and the ROOT 5 and 6 BAR CHORDS is that the 6th string should not be played when you strum the chord. Because of this factor, ROOT 4 BAR CHORDS are slightly confining for the rhythm guitarist. Every lead guitarist, however, should be thoroughly familiar with these chords.

Examine the note chart at the right:

The letters (D, Eb, E, F, etc.) stand for the notes produced by the 4th string at various frets. For example, the 4th string open produces the note D; when you push down behind the 2nd fret the 4th string produces E; behind the 3rd fret the 4th string produces F; etc. Go up and down the 4th string a few times playing and saying out loud the note each fret produces. After you're familiar with these notes, start working on the first ROOT 4 BAR CHORD: the major chord.

NOTES PRODUCED
BY THE 4TH STRING

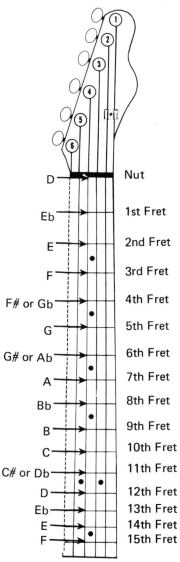

D	Nut
Eb	1st Fret
E	2nd Fret
F	3rd Fret
F# or Gb	4th Fret
G	5th Fret
G# or Ab	6th Fret
A	7th Fret
Bb	8th Fret
B	9th Fret
C	10th Fret
C# or Db	11th Fret
D	12th Fret
Eb	13th Fret
E	14th Fret
F	15th Fret

THE MAJOR CHORD

Examine and play this first ROOT 4 CHORD. You must take care *not* to play the 6th string when you strum the chord as it is indicated by a broken line.

D CHORD

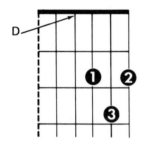

With this chord, the open 4th string is the root. With a bar you can play this chord formation at any fret. This chord is a little awkward to finger with a bar but should be studied nonetheless.

MOVABLE MAJOR CHORD

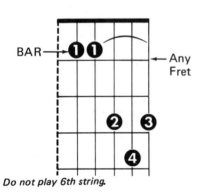

Do not play 6th string.

As this major chord is a ROOT 4 BAR CHORD, the letter name of the chord is determined by the position the bar takes on the 4th string.

When the bar is behind the 2nd fret you have an E chord; behind the 3rd fret you have an F chord; behind the 5th fret a G chord; etc.

NOTES PRODUCED
BY THE 4TH STRING

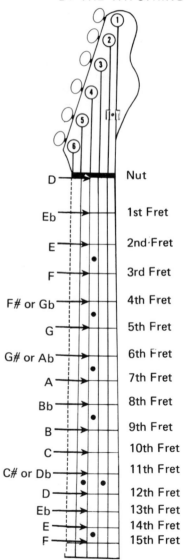

D	Nut
Eb	1st Fret
E	2nd Fret
F	3rd Fret
F# or Gb	4th Fret
G	5th Fret
G# or Ab	6th Fret
A	7th Fret
Bb	8th Fret
B	9th Fret
C	10th Fret
C# or Db	11th Fret
D	12th Fret
Eb	13th Fret
E	14th Fret
F	15th Fret

Make this bar chord behind any fret.

Play the following progression using this new chord with ROOT 5 and ROOT 6 BAR CHORDS. Interestingly enough, the bar remains behind the 3rd fret for the entire progression. Practice it until you can play it very fast.

CHORD PROGRESSION

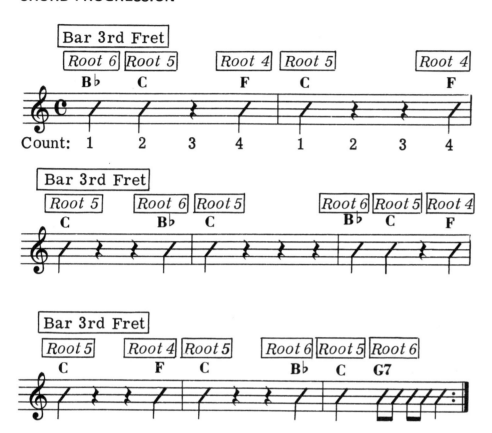

THE 6th CHORD

By removing the 3rd finger, you convert the D chord into a D 6th chord:

D 6TH CHORD

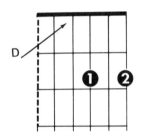

Play the movable 6th chord at a few different frets.

MOVABLE 6TH CHORD

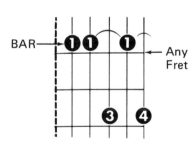

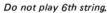

Do not play 6th string.

As this new 6th chord is a ROOT 4 BAR CHORD, the letter name of the chord is determined by the position the bar takes on the 4th string.

When the bar is behind the 2nd fret, you have an E 6th chord; behind the 3rd fret you have an F 6th chord; behind the 5th fret a G 6th chord; etc.

Make this bar chord behind any fret.

NOTES PRODUCED
BY THE 4TH STRING

D	Nut
Eb	1st Fret
E	2nd Fret
F	3rd Fret
F# or Gb	4th Fret
G	5th Fret
G# or Ab	6th Fret
A	7th Fret
Bb	8th Fret
B	9th Fret
C	10th Fret
C# or Db	11th Fret
D	12th Fret
Eb	13th Fret
E	14th Fret
F	15th Fret

THE 7th CHORD

A slight but significant alteration in fingering changes the D chord into a D 7th chord:

D 7TH CHORD

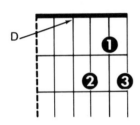

By using this chord formation with a bar, you can play over fifteen new 7th chords! This is a very useful chord so spend some time with it.

MOVABLE 7TH CHORD

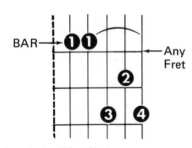

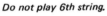

Do not play 6th string.

NOTES PRODUCED
BY THE 4TH STRING

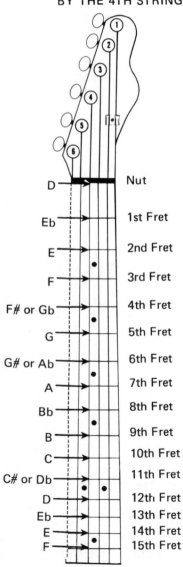

As this 7th chord is a ROOT 4 BAR CHORD, the letter name of the chord is determined by the position the bar takes on the 4th string.

When the bar is behind the 2nd fret, you have an E 7th chord; behind the 3rd fret you have an F 7th chord; behind the 5th fret you have a G 7th chord; etc.

Make this bar chord behind any fret.

76

One of the more effective uses of this new 7th chord is to use it in combination with the ROOT 6 7th chord. Say you're playing a song where you have a G 7th chord called for:

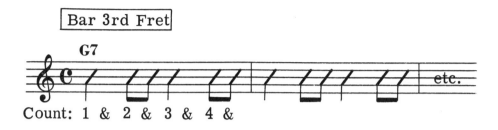

Rather than playing the ROOT 6 7th chord over and over, you can insert the ROOT 4 7th chord to add interest:

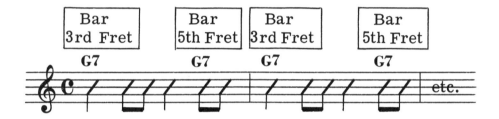

THE MAJOR 7th CHORD

By moving the finger on the 2nd string down one fret, the D chord becomes a D Maj. 7th chord. The easiest fingering is to bar the first three strings with the 1st finger.

D MAJOR 7TH CHORD

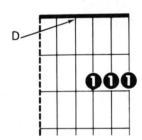

By using this chord formation with a bar, you can play a new series of major 7th chords.

MOVABLE MAJOR 7TH CHORD

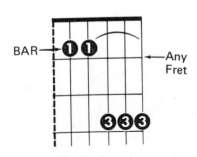

Do not play 6th string.

As this major 7th chord is a ROOT 4 BAR CHORD, the letter name of the chord is determined by the position the bar takes on the 4th string. When the bar is behind the 2nd fret, you have an E Maj. 7th chord; be-

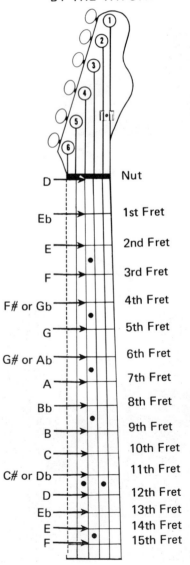

NOTES PRODUCED
BY THE 4TH STRING

D	Nut
Eb	1st Fret
E	2nd Fret
F	3rd Fret
F# or Gb	4th Fret
G	5th Fret
G# or Ab	6th Fret
A	7th Fret
Bb	8th Fret
B	9th Fret
C	10th Fret
C# or Db	11th Fret
D	12th Fret
Eb	13th Fret
E	14th Fret
F	15th Fret

hind the 3rd fret you have an F Maj. 7th chord; behind the 5th fret a G Maj. 7th chord; etc.

Make this bar chord behind any fret.

Play the following blues progression using all the ROOT 4 BAR CHORDS presented thus far. The progression illustrates how these four chords can be used together as well as how and where to locate them.

BLUES IN Eb

THE MINOR CHORD

Compare the fingering and sound of the D minor chord to the ROOT 4 D chord:

D MINOR CHORD

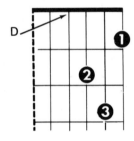

When you strum these chords, do not play the 6th string.

D CHORD

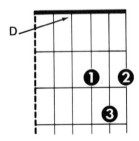

Try to get the difference between these two chords in your ears as well as your fingers. By using the D minor chord formation with a bar, you can play a new set of minor chords.

MOVABLE MINOR CHORD

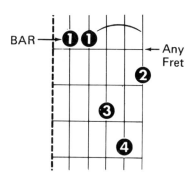

BAR

Any Fret

Do not play 6th string.

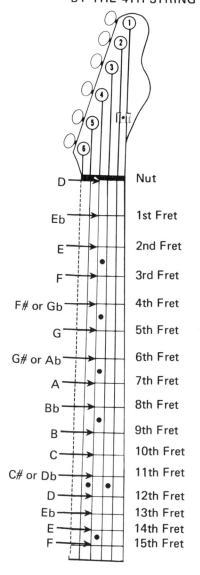

D	Nut
Eb	1st Fret
E	2nd Fret
F	3rd Fret
F# or Gb	4th Fret
G	5th Fret
G# or Ab	6th Fret
A	7th Fret
Bb	8th Fret
B	9th Fret
C	10th Fret
C# or Db	11th Fret
D	12th Fret
Eb	13th Fret
E	14th Fret
F	15th Fret

As this new minor chord is a ROOT 4 BAR CHORD, the letter name of the chord is determined by the position the bar takes on the 4th string.

When the bar is behind the 2nd fret, you have an E minor chord; behind the 3rd fret you have an F minor chord; behind the 5th fret a G minor chord; etc.

Make this minor chord behind any fret.

The new ROOT 4 minor chord combines with the ROOT 6 and ROOT 5 BAR CHORDS to make up the familiar turn-around progression. After you master the progression starting at the 5th fret, play it starting at the 7th fret and later at the 8th fret for further practice. This progression should definitely be played on the slow side.

TURN-AROUND PROGRESSION

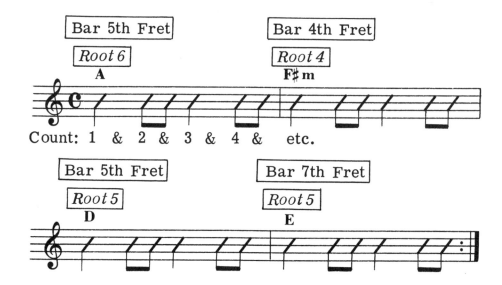

81

THE MINOR 6th CHORD

By removing the 3rd finger from the D minor chord, you form a D minor 6th chord:

D MINOR 6TH CHORD

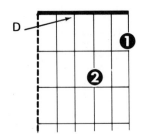

Used with a bar, the D minor 6th chord formation adds about fifteen new minor 6th chords to your vocabulary!

MOVABLE MINOR 6TH CHORD

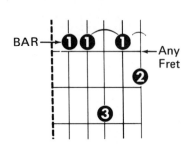

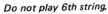

Do not play 6th string.

As this minor 6th chord is a ROOT 4 BAR CHORD, the letter name of the chord is determined by the position the bar takes on the 4th string.

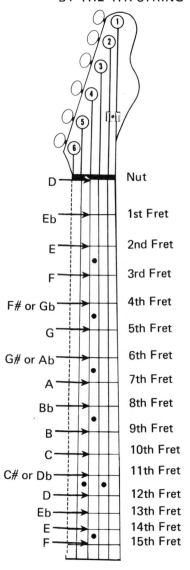

NOTES PRODUCED
BY THE 4TH STRING

D	Nut
Eb	1st Fret
E	2nd Fret
F	3rd Fret
F# or Gb	4th Fret
G	5th Fret
G# or Ab	6th Fret
A	7th Fret
Bb	8th Fret
B	9th Fret
C	10th Fret
C# or Db	11th Fret
D	12th Fret
Eb	13th Fret
E	14th Fret
F	15th Fret

When the bar is behind the 2nd fret, you have an E minor 6th chord; behind the 3rd fret you have an F minor 6th chord; behind the 5th fret a G minor 6th chord; etc.

Make this new minor 6th chord behind any fret.

THE MINOR 7th CHORD

By barring the 1st and 2nd strings with the 1st finger, the D minor chord becomes a D minor 7th chord:

D MINOR 7TH CHORD

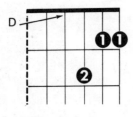

By using the D minor 7th chord formation with a bar you can play a new set of minor 7th chords. Play this new movable minor 7th chord at a few different frets.

MOVABLE MINOR 7TH CHORD

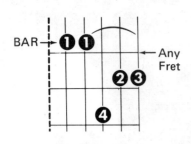

Do not play 6th string.

NOTES PRODUCED
BY THE 4TH STRING

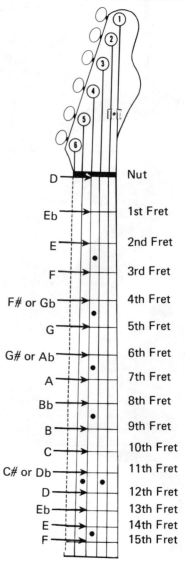

D	Nut
Eb	1st Fret
E	2nd Fret
F	3rd Fret
F# or Gb	4th Fret
G	5th Fret
G# or Ab	6th Fret
A	7th Fret
Bb	8th Fret
B	9th Fret
C	10th Fret
C# or Db	11th Fret
D	12th Fret
Eb	13th Fret
E	14th Fret
F	15th Fret

As this new minor 7th chord is a ROOT 4 BAR CHORD, the letter name of the chord is determined by the position the bar takes on the 4th string.

When the bar is behind the 2nd fret, you have an E minor 7th chord; behind the 3rd fret you have an F minor 7th chord; behind the 5th fret a G minor 7th chord; etc.

Make this new bar chord behind any fret.

THE DIMINISHED CHORD *

The ROOT 4 diminished chord is by far the most popular diminished chord used by today's rock guitarists. This chord can only be played effectively as a movable chord starting at the 1st fret. Play the chord at a few different frets taking care not to play the 5th and 6th strings when you strum it.

MOVABLE DIMINISHED CHORD

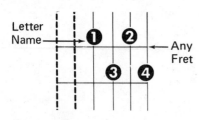

Do not play 5th or 6th strings.

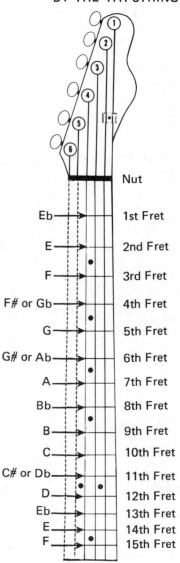

As this new diminished chord is a ROOT 4 CHORD, the letter name of the chord is determined by the position the 1st finger takes on the 4th string. The location of this chord is a little different than the other chords we've studied so you'll have to take extra care.

When the 1st finger is behind the 2nd fret, you have an E diminished chord; behind the 3rd fret you have an F diminished chord; behind the 5th fret a G diminished chord; etc.

Make this new diminished chord behind any fret.

To give you a better understanding of where the diminished chord is used, play this next popular progression. I have purposely avoided indicating whether a chord is a ROOT 6, ROOT 5, or a ROOT 4 CHORD. The fret indications should tell you this.

POPULAR PROGRESSION

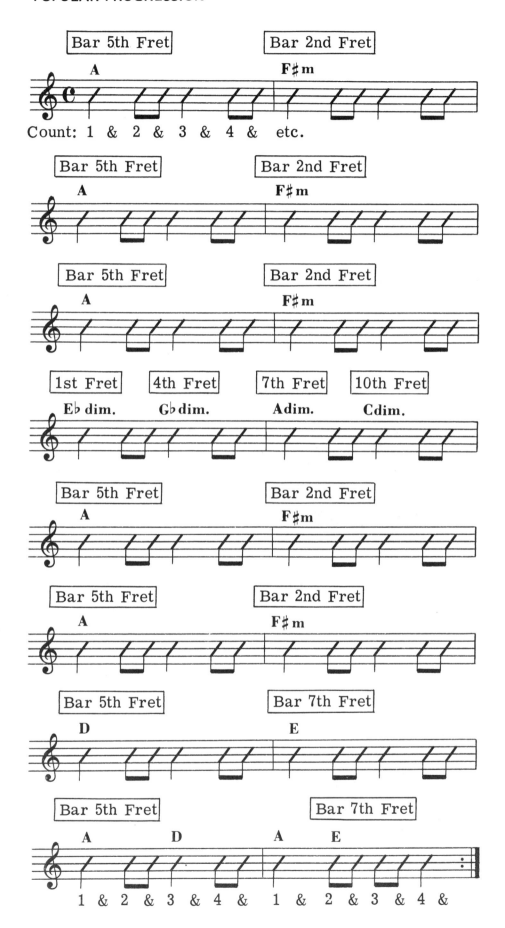

THE AUGMENTED CHORD *

The augmented chord is one of the most unusual rock chords you'll have to play. Finger and play this E augmented chord taking care not to play the 5th and 6th strings when you strum the chord.

E AUGMENTED CHORD

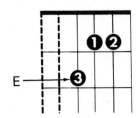

The movable augmented chord is quite simple to form. As with the diminished chord, do not play the 5th and 6th strings when you strum the chord.

MOVABLE AUGMENTED CHORD

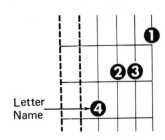

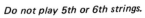

Do not play 5th or 6th strings.

The letter name of this chord depends on the location of the 4th finger. When the 4th finger is behind the 3rd fret, you have an F augmented chord; when the 4th finger is behind the 5th fret, the letter of the chord is G augmented; behind the 7th fret an A augmented chord.

NOTES PRODUCED BY THE 4TH STRING

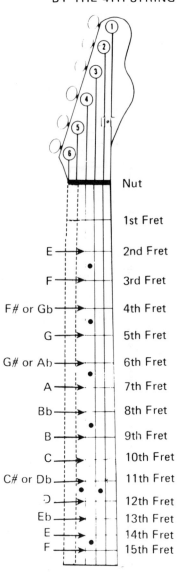

Form this chord behind any fret.

Often you will find the augmented chord abbreviated aug. or simply +
and occasionally 7+5. Thus, A augmented, A aug., A+, and A7+5 all refer
to the same chord.

THE MAJOR 7th CHORD *

Now we'll work on the most popular major 7th chord used by rock guitarists. Here it is in open position. As with the previous two chords, do not play the 5th and 6th strings when you strum the chord.

F MAJOR 7TH CHORD

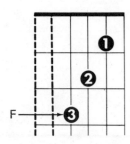

The F major 7th chord can be easily converted into a movable chord. You'll have to stretch your left hand fingers a little to play this one.

MOVABLE MAJOR 7TH CHORD

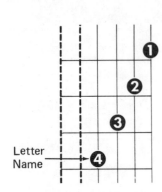

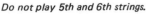

Do not play 5th and 6th strings.

As this major 7th chord is a ROOT 4 CHORD, the letter name of the chord is determined by the position the 4th finger takes on the 4th string.

Locating the chord by the position of the 4th finger is a little unusual so make a note of this.

NOTES PRODUCED
BY THE 4TH STRING

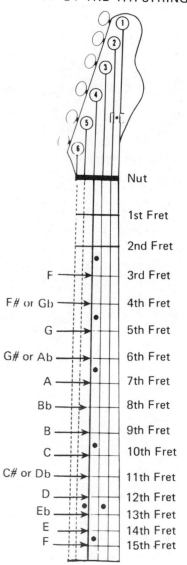

	Nut
	1st Fret
	2nd Fret
F →	3rd Fret
F# or Gb →	4th Fret
G →	5th Fret
G# or Ab →	6th Fret
A →	7th Fret
Bb →	8th Fret
B →	9th Fret
C →	10th Fret
C# or Db →	11th Fret
D →	12th Fret
Eb →	13th Fret
E →	14th Fret
F →	15th Fret

When the 4th finger is behind the 5th fret, you have a G Maj. 7th chord; behind the 7th fret you have an A Maj. 7th chord; behind the 9th fret a B Maj. 7th chord; etc.

Form this movable major 7th chord behind any fret.

For an alternate fingering of this major 7th chord that many rock guitarists prefer, wrap the thumb of the left hand around the neck of the guitar and push down the 6th string with it. At the same time allow the thumb to touch and dampen the 5th string. With the major 7th chord fingered this way, play all six strings when you strum the chord. Play it at a few different frets.

MOVABLE MAJOR 7TH CHORD

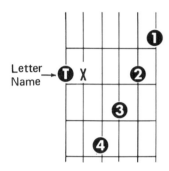

Letter Name →

Damp the 5th string with the thumb.

Although the fingering is very similar to the last ROOT 4 major 7th chord we studied, this is a ROOT 6 chord. The letter name of the chord is indicated by the position the thumb takes on the 6th string.

When the thumb is behind the 2nd fret you have an F# Maj. 7th chord; behind the 3rd fret you have a G Maj. 7th chord; behind the 5th fret an A Maj. 7th chord; etc.

Form this new major 7th chord behind any fret.

NOTES PRODUCED BY THE 6TH STRING

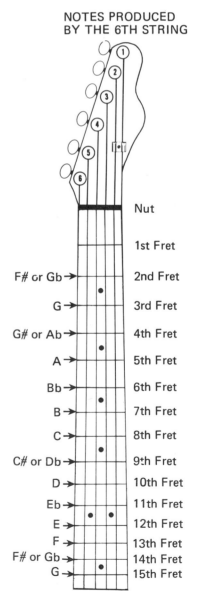

	Nut
	1st Fret
F# or Gb →	2nd Fret
G →	3rd Fret
G# or Ab →	4th Fret
A →	5th Fret
Bb →	6th Fret
B →	7th Fret
C →	8th Fret
C# or Db →	9th Fret
D →	10th Fret
Eb →	11th Fret
E →	12th Fret
F →	13th Fret
F# or Gb →	14th Fret
G →	15th Fret

THE EXERCISE USING ROOT 4 BAR CHORDS

The following exercise makes use of all the ROOT 4 CHORDS presented in this book. Practice this exercise until you can play it with ease. Name the chords out loud as you play them and the exercise will not only strengthen the muscles in your left hand, but add to your ability to recall these rock chords as well.

Remember not to play the strings indicated by broken lines.

EXERCISE

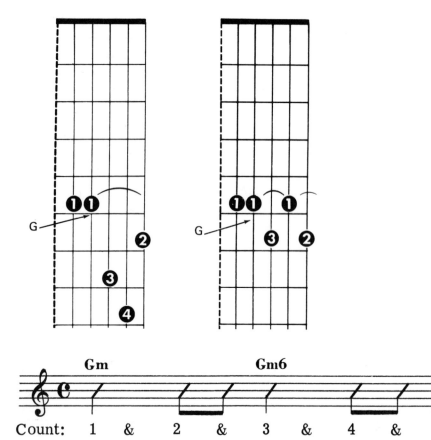

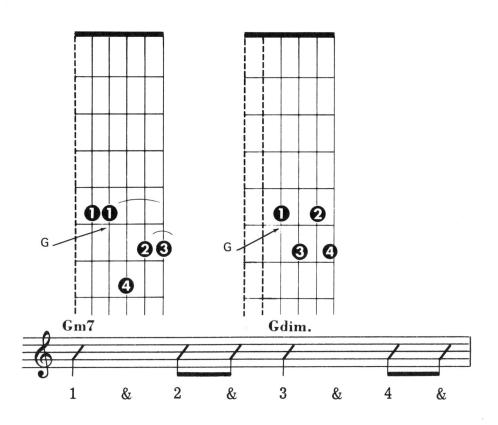

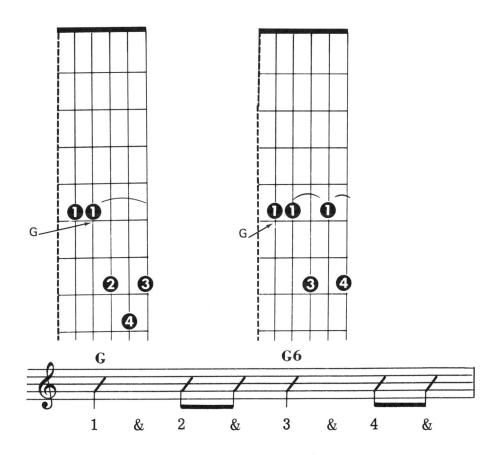

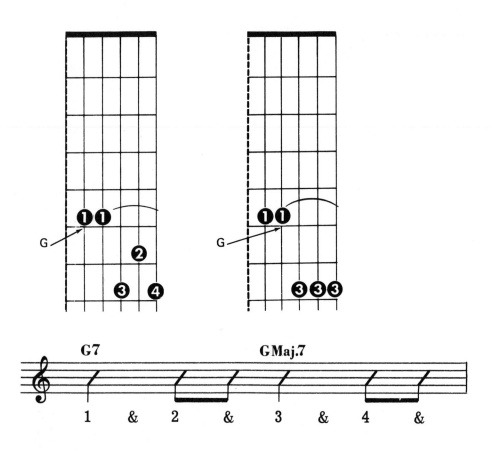

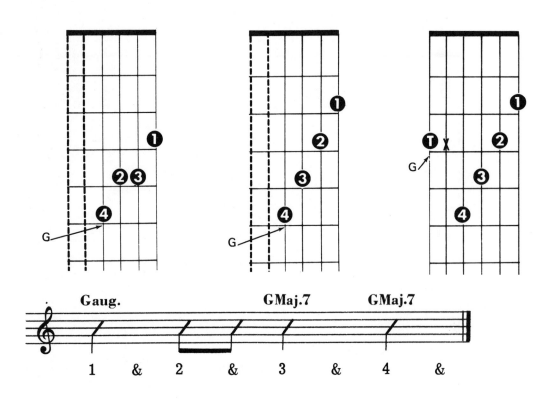

You now know every chord used by today's professional rock guitarists. With all these hundreds of chord formations at your fingertips, it is often difficult to decide which chord formation is best to use in a particular situation. (For example, which of the six C Major chord formations would you use to begin a song with?) Here are a few points to consider when choosing a chord formation:

1. Use chord formations that compliment the mood of the song. Certain blues are more effective using low, deep chords. Up-tempo R & B is fun to play above the fifth fret. Many slow songs sound best using all open chords.

2. Use the chord formation that is closest physically to the previous chord used.

3. Consider using more than one formation of the same chord. If a song stays on one chord for a long time, you might change chord formation to add interest.

4. Always make your chords so that every string rings with clarity. Don't slouch. Every note counts.

APPENDIX A: CHORD CATALOG

chords with root (letter name) on 6th string

E MAJOR CHORD
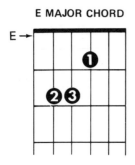

E 6TH CHORD
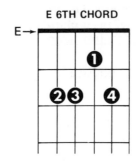

E 7TH CHORD
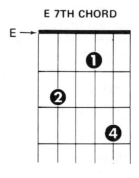

MOVABLE MAJOR CHORD
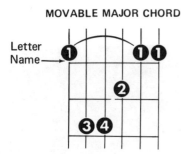

MOVABLE 6TH CHORD
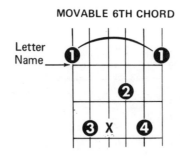

MOVABLE 7TH CHORD
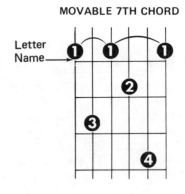

E AUG. 9TH CHORD
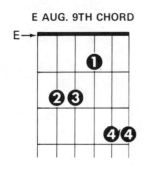

E 9TH CHORD
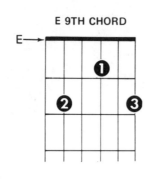

E MINOR CHORD
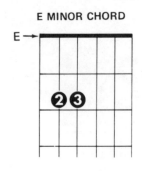

MOVABLE AUG. 9TH CHORD
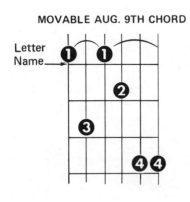

MOVABLE 9TH CHORD
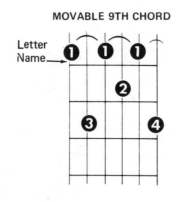

MOVABLE MINOR CHORD
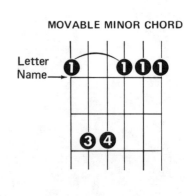

E MINOR 6TH CHORD

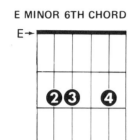

E MINOR 7TH CHORD

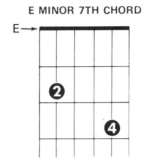

E MINOR 9TH CHORD

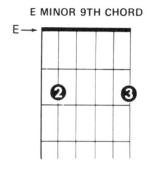

MOVABLE MINOR 6TH CHORD

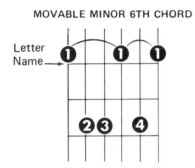

MOVABLE MINOR 7TH CHORD

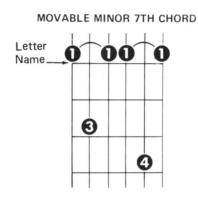

MOVABLE MINOR 9TH CHORD

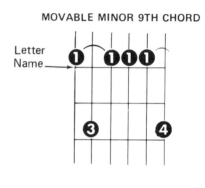

E DIMINISHED CHORD

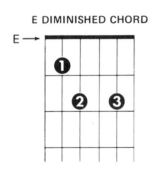

G MAJOR CHORD

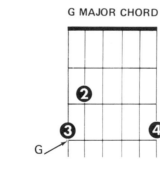

G 6TH CHORD

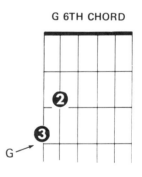

MOVABLE DIMINISHED CHORD

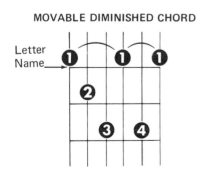

MOVABLE 6TH CHORD

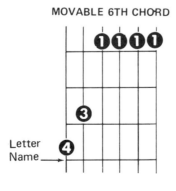

MOVABLE MAJOR CHORD

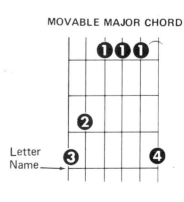

G 7TH CHORD

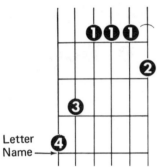

MOVABLE 7TH CHORD

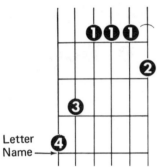

MOVABLE MAJOR 7TH CHORD

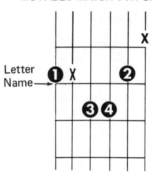

chords with root (letter name) on 5th string

A MAJOR CHORD

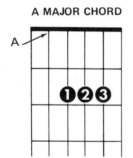

A 6TH CHORD

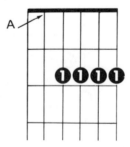

A 7TH CHORD

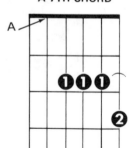

MOVABLE MAJOR CHORD

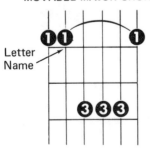

MOVABLE 6TH CHORD

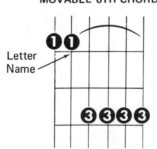

MOVABLE 7TH CHORD

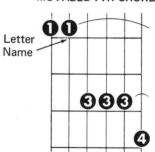

98

A MAJOR 7TH CHORD

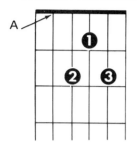

A MINOR CHORD

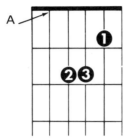

A MINOR 6TH CHORD

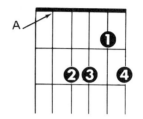

MOVABLE MAJOR 7TH CHORD

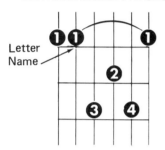

MOVABLE MINOR CHORD

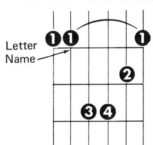

MOVABLE MINOR 6TH CHORD

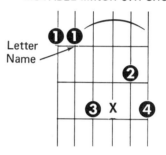

A MINOR 7TH CHORD

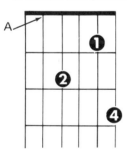

C MAJOR CHORD

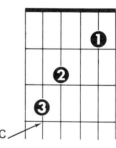

MOVABLE MINOR 7TH CHORD

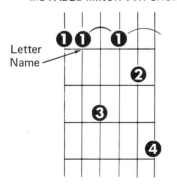

MOVABLE DIMINISHED CHORD

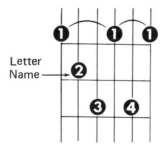

MOVABLE MAJOR CHORD

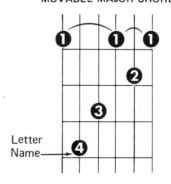

C MAJOR 7TH CHORD

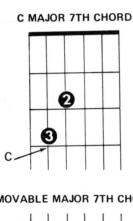

C 7TH CHORD

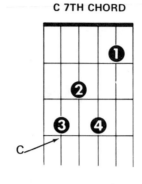

MOVABLE MAJOR 7TH CHORD

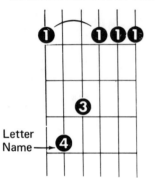

MOVABLE 7TH CHORD

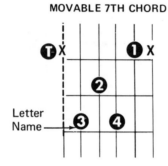

MOVABLE 9TH CHORD

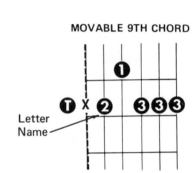

chords with root (letter name) on 4th string

D MAJOR CHORD

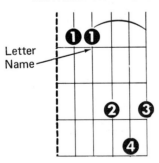

D 6TH CHORD

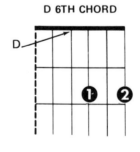

D 7TH CHORD

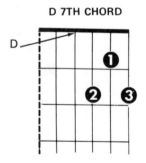

MOVABLE MAJOR CHORD

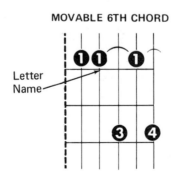

MOVABLE 6TH CHORD

MOVABLE 7TH CHORD

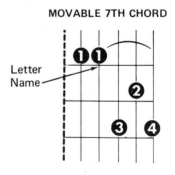

D MAJOR 7TH CHORD

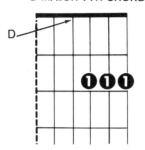

D MINOR CHORD

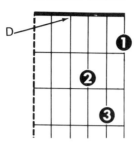

D MINOR 6TH CHORD

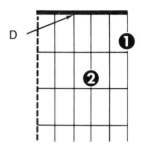

MOVABLE MAJOR 7TH CHORD

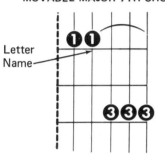

MOVABLE MINOR CHORD

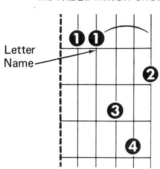

MOVABLE MINOR 6TH CHORD

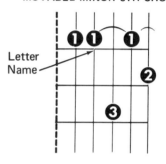

D MINOR 7TH CHORD

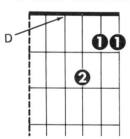

E AUGMENTED CHORD

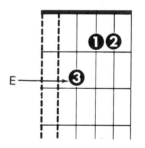

MOVABLE MINOR 7TH CHORD

MOVABLE DIMINISHED CHORD

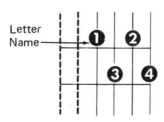

MOVABLE AUGMENTED CHORD

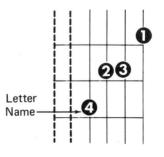

F MAJOR 7TH CHORD

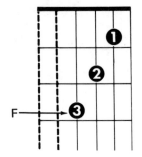

F

MOVABLE MAJOR 7TH CHORD

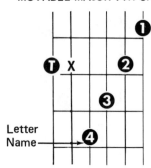

Letter
Name

APPENDIX B: GUITAR TUNING

TUNING INSTRUCTIONS

Every musician, sooner or later, has to come to grips with the problem of tuning his instrument. When you're playing along and something just doesn't sound right, you can almost bet that your guitar is out of tune. The more you play with a tuned guitar, the easier you can tell when it is out of tune. The person who suffers the most from an out-of-tune instrument is you and your ears. So keep your guitar in tune! Let's begin.

There's more than one way to tune a guitar. In the beginning, it's easiest to use a guitar pitch pipe. When in tune, each string on the guitar produces a specific note that corresponds to one of the notes of the pitch pipe.

Here are some helpful hints.

Before starting to tune, experiment with your tuning pegs by turning them one way and then the other, to see which way tightens the string and which way loosens it. (Remember, tightening makes the pitch go *up,* loosening makes the pitch go *down.*) This will also help you to determine how much to turn the peg to get the pitch you want.

Try to keep your guitar in playing position while you are tuning up. You may have to lean forward or move the guitar to see which peg (also called tuning gear) is attached to which string, but after a while you will memorize the sequence. As a quick check, you can follow the string with a right hand finger down to its peg.

Blow a note on the pitch pipe. (The notes are marked on the pipe, corresponding to the open strings of the guitar — E A D G B E.) As you are blowing (and listening) pluck the corresponding string on the guitar and determine whether it is higher or lower than the note you are producing on the pipe. Turn the peg until the plucked string sounds the same as the sound of the pipe.

For those of you who are using a piano to tune your guitar, the 1st string on the guitar (high E) corresponds to the E above middle C. The low E string produces a sound two octaves below that. Here is a diagram which shows you how to find the notes you'll need on the piano.

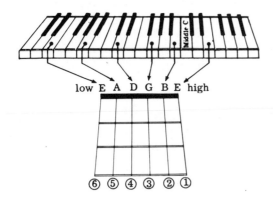

When tuning to the piano, hold down the sustaining pedal (the one on the right) with your foot. The note will ring longer, making it easier for you to match it up with the string you are tuning.

If you have neither pitch pipe nor piano, you can still get your guitar in tune. It's a little tricky, but definitely worth learning. There will be many times in the future that you'll have to tune your guitar without any other instruments around to tune to.

Start by assuming that your low E (6th string) is fairly on pitch. If it seems too high (tight) loosen the string a bit; if it seems too low (loose and buzzing) turn the peg to tighten the string a little.

When the 6th string sounds all right to you, fret it (press it down) on the fifth fret, using a left hand finger. At the same time, pluck that string with your right hand thumb or pick. The note you get will be an A, the correct note for the A (5th) string. Tune the 5th string to that sound.

When the 5th string is in tune with the 6th string, fret it at the 5th fret. This will give you the correct note to tune your D (4th) string to.

When that is in tune, fret it (the 4th string) at the 5th fret, and you'll get a G note. Tune the 3rd string to that note.

To tune the B (2nd) string, press down the G string at the 4th fret. This will give you a B, so tune the 2nd string to that note.

Finally, fret the 2nd string at the 5th fret to tune the 1st string. When you've done all that, play the two outer strings together. They should sound the same even though they are two octaves apart. Strum some of the chords you know to further check your tuning. You might have to go over your tuning a few times until you get the right sounds.

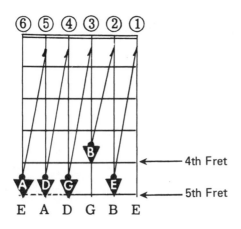

When you're playing in a group, you will tune your guitar to the other instruments in the band. If there is a piano or organ, everyone in the group will tune to that since it has a fixed pitch. Otherwise, choose the instrument that is closest to being perfectly in tune and use that as your standard. The nicest things can happen when several instruments get in tune and play together.

GUITARS·SPEAKERS·AMPLIFIERS

by Dan Armstrong

The guitar has been around, in one form or another, for well over three-hundred years. It has been the backbone of American country and folk music since that kind of music began. But with the discovery and development of the electric guitar in the 1930's, a great new musical voice appeared. In the mid-1950's the guitar explosion began, propelling it to the foreground of today's music.

The guitar has evolved from a crudely amplified box to a highly sophisticated electronic instrument, capable of producing an almost unlimited compass of melodies, harmonies, tone colors, rhythms and musical expression at orchestral level.

Today, pop-rock guitarists use the instrument in three rather distinct ways: to provide the predominant instrumental voice (lead guitar); to supply chords, harmonies and rhythmic foundation (rhythm guitar); and to indicate an overall harmonic pattern and direction by providing the roots of the chords, and by supplying a rhythmic pulse (bass guitar).

With millions of guitars for the player to choose from, it's difficult for you to know which instrument will best serve your needs. The following information is an attempt to aid in your search for the best equipment.

Evaluating the Instrument

Sound: Virtually every well known rock player is identifiable by his personal sound, whether he's playing solos or musical figures which are incidental to the vocal lines. For example, some players want the guitar to sound as much like a human voice as possible. Others prefer what can best be called a "dirty" sound. There are perhaps as many individual sounds as there are players. A good guitar should produce the sound that the player wants to hear. It's that player's guitar, as well as his own style and personality, that produce his particular sound.

The basic consideration in choosing an instrument, then, is sound. The guitar should be capable of producing clear, bright highs and solid, distinct notes in the low range. And each note of a chord should speak with equal clarity. The guitar should speak strongly, not strained as if it's trying too hard to produce its sound. ⟫→

EARLY ELECTRIC GUITAR 1935

SOLID BODY GUITAR

Feel: Another important consideration in choosing an instrument is the way it feels. Does it feel sturdy? Does it feel as though a maximum of care and craftsmanship went into its manufacture? Does the neck feel right in your hand? Does the instrument balance nicely? Or is it too heavy (or too light) on one end, so that it's difficult to hold in playing position?

Action:* Good action is important. The strings should feel comfortable under your fingers and should press down to the fingerboard easily at every fret, from first to last. The body of the instrument should be shaped so that even the highest notes can be played with ease. The strings should be properly spaced, so that both picking and fretting are easy and comfortable. The location and design of the bridge should not hamper picking.

Neck: The neck of the guitar must be adjustable. It's greatly affected by string tension. High tension may cause the neck to bow upward and low tension will allow a reverse warp, or downward bowing. If the neck cannot be adjusted to compensate for these conditions, the guitar is likely to become completely unplayable. It's not advisable for the average player to attempt to adjust his own guitar neck. The adjustment is more complicated than it may seem and should be done by an experienced repair man.

NECK ADJUSTMENT MECHANICS
Rod imbedded in neck at predetermined reverse curve. Tightening nut (1) pushes ends of rod closer together, resulting in neck tension opposite of string pull.

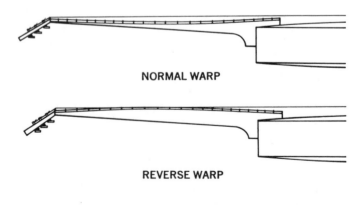

NORMAL WARP

REVERSE WARP

* There will be complete discussion of problems with action later in this article.

Bridge: Another essential is an adjustable bridge. There must be provision in the bridge for raising or lowering both the bass and treble sides in order to obtain the proper string height. The bridge must also be adjustable back and forth so that the string lengths may be altered to insure proper intonation. Some bridges have individual string "saddles" which can be adjusted back and forth to obtain the ideal length of each string. The trend seems to be toward all-metal bridges. The bridge, of whatever type, should be of sturdy construction and seated securely.

Pickups: The pickups should be securely mounted and should be adjustable so that portions of the pickup, or the entire pickup, can be brought closer to the quieter strings and farther from the louder ones by means of individual adjustment screws. Generally the high E and the G strings do not equal the others in volume. In other words, the sounds produced by the strings should be evenly balanced by the pickups. Beware of pickups that have ornamental "adjustment screws" which serve no function other than deceiving the buyer! Pickups made this way are probably less valuable than pickups which don't even attempt to appear adjustable. One pickup, strategically placed, is sometimes sufficient, but two pickups (though seldom three) are preferred by most players. No one seems to have found a satisfactory way to use four pickups.

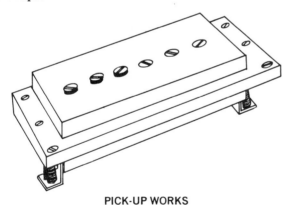

PICK-UP WORKS

Controls: The guitar should have a switch that activates any pickup or combination of pickups. (This does not apply, of course, to single pickup instruments); at least one volume control that gives a smooth, gradual increase or decrease in volume; and at least one equally smooth-tapered tone control. Some instruments have more controls than these. Avoid instruments with a confusing array of dials, toggle-switches and little wheels sprouting from all over the guitar. The

ILLUSTRATIONS BY HOWARD BERELSON

purpose of controls is to produce the desired changes in sound, quickly and efficiently, not to adorn the guitar.

Body: Electric guitars fall into three categories with respect to body type: solid body, semi-hollow body and hollow body. The solid-body does not vibrate along with the strings. It has a tendency to sustain notes extremely well, thereby producing the most electronic sound of the three styles. A true hollow-body guitar has considerably less sustaining power and a more natural tone, but also tends to produce undesirable feedback** at high volume. A semi-hollow guitar combines the best features of both solid and hollow-body guitars, allowing a reasonable amount of sustaining power, yet retaining a more natural, less electronic sound, with little feedback.

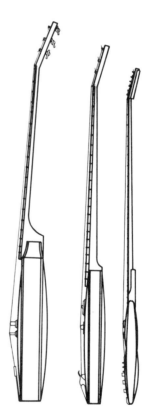

DIFFERENT THICKNESSES OF GUITAR BODIES

Appearance: Many players consider appearance to be an important factor in choosing a guitar. Since appearance is an entirely subjective matter, I can make no recommendations in this area. However, my experience indicates that those who consider appearance a prime factor are either

----

** *Some rock players use feedback for desired effects. Refer to section on Accessories.*

non-professional players, or the professionals who have not yet attained fame. Some of the most widely respected players I know have some of the raggediest guitars I have ever seen—but they keep them adjusted to perfection.

Case: The guitar's case should be one in which the instrument fits securely and which affords maximum protection from weather, temperature and abuse.

When in doubt as to which guitar to buy, consider what your favorite well-known player uses, or consult people in the folowing order: *1* the best player you can find to talk to; *2* your local repairman; *3* your guitar teacher (if he's not also a salesman); *4* yourself and your own judgment, and *5* your dealer.

Accessories

There's a trend toward an increasing array of accessory equipment for the rock player to use for producing various electronic effects.

GUITAR WITH ACCESSORIES

Reverberation: One of the most widely used effects is reverberation, which creates the effect of playing in a big auditorium. Most recognized

groups prefer not to use reverb in stage appearances, striving instead for a more real, live sound. Good amps are available with or without reverb. For the amp without built-in reverb there are also good auxiliary units which can be used in conjunction with any amplifier.

Tape Echo: Tape Echo is used to produce a shimmery, less mechanical effect than 'spring type' reverb. The sound is first recorded on a tape, then played back immediately—the effect being a delayed reproduction of sound. The longer the delay between recording and playback, the more pronounced is the repetition of the sound. If this delay is increased enough, the effect is a true echo, so that a note or chord is repeated over and over until it gradually diminishes and disappears.

Tremolo: Another effect incorporated into many of today's amplifiers is tremolo, a fluctuation in volume which can be controlled in speed and depth. Tremolo, if used sparingly, is an interesting effect, especially on sustained notes or chords.

Vibrato: Some amplifiers feature vibrato, a variable fluctuation in pitch, produced electronically. Most players find that vibrato is more effectively produced by bending the strings in playing rather than producing it in a robot manner by the amplifier.

Vibrato Tailpiece: Vibrato tailpieces seem to be quite a fine idea. It's unfortunate, however, that there are none that work well. Their purpose, of course, is to raise and lower the pitch of all the strings together. A successful device has yet to be discovered and, therefore, the better players not only avoid the use of the vibrato tailpieces but prefer not to have them on their guitars at all. These gadgets, by their nature, cause the guitar to untune in several ways:

a. The string tension, when changed by this tailpiece, is not increased or decreased evenly on all strings, causing chords in anything but the neutral position to be noticeably out of tune.

b. Since it is a non-fixed tailpiece and is delicately balanced between the pull of the strings and a counteracting spring in the tailpiece, the tuning of one string will affect all the others, making it more difficult to tune the guitar initially and to keep it in tune subsequently.

c. Friction in the mechanism itself seldom allows the strings to return to the correct pitch they were tuned to originally.

Flexible strings can produce the vibrato effect nicely and far more efficiently than any vibrato mechanism.

Treble booster: Treble-boosting greatly intensifies the high overtones produced by the guitar. It's an electronic 'valve' through which only the highest sounding tones can pass. Since the treble booster does not actually produce highs, but only accentuates those already present, its value with some instruments is doubtful.

Bass-booster: A bass-booster is a treble booster in reverse. It's a similar electronic valve, allowing only low-frequency tones to pass through. It eliminates the high overtones and thereby intensifies the lows.

Fuzz and Distortion: There's a rumor that the use of fuzz as an effect began when an amplifier speaker blew at a recording session and the resulting distortion so delighted everyone that they recorded the sound. Distortion isn't always desirable. Most fuzz-producers are capable of distorting only one note at a time and therefore sound best when used to play a single-note line. Powerful pickups, adjusted to bass control setting, seem to work best with the fuzz-producers. Fuzz is most exciting when played on the low strings or on a bass guitar.

Foot-pedal Controls: Some players use foot-pedal controls to considerable advantage. Pedal volume controls act like an automobile accelerator. With the pedal fully depressed, the volume is maximum and, with the pedal fully let up, the volume is lowered to minimum, or off. Often incorporated in these pedals is a tone-changing feature, allowing extreme changes from bass to treble tones, by means of side-to-side motion of the same pedal. Therefore, up and down for volume changes and side-to-side for tone changes.

Feedback: Until recently, feedback has been an undesirable quality of the electric guitar. Feedback is a "loop" of sound produced when the vibrations of the strings are carried through the pickup to the amplifier and reproduced as sound by the loud speaker. That sound reaches the guitar and causes the strings to keep vibrating. As this cycle continues, the strings are caused to vibrate steadily harder and the sound becomes steadily

louder until the amplifier reaches its limits and a whining noise results. Controlled feedback is a useful effect. It limits the feedback to a certain level and achieves a wild electronic effect.

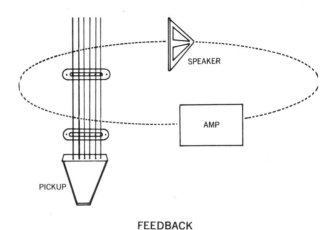

FEEDBACK

Stereo Wiring: Some guitars are wired so that each pickup may be played through a separate amplifier or separate channels in the same amplifier. This means that one pickup may go into the amplifier through a fuzz or distortion device and the other may go through a treble-booster, bass-booster, reverb unit, etc. Each may be separately controlled, allowing a great many effects.

Typical Problems of Action and Intonation

Poor Action: The guitar's action (the relationship of the strings to the fingerboard) should be low enough to permit relative ease of playing. In order to have the extremely low, easy action sought by most of today's players, these factors are critical:

   a. An absolutely straight neck

   b. Frets of absolutely regular height

   c. Nut and bridge of proper height

   d. At least 1/16th-inch clearance between pickup and strings.

Below is a diagram of a guitar adjusted for ideal action.

IDEAL ACTION

Poor Intonation: Intonation refers to the tuning of the guitar and the ability to have its strings in tune with themselves from the first fret to the last. The major cause of poor intonation is poor strings—those that are badly made or excessively worn. New strings sound best and feel best, and certainly contribute to consistent tuning. Always use the best quality strings you can afford and change them often (at least once a month). Don't wait until they break!

Another common cause of poor intonation is an improperly-located bridge. Theoretically, the bridge is located the same distance from the twelfth fret as from the twelfth fret to the nut. In practice it doesn't work out quite that way. Here's how to determine ideal bridge locations.

Start with the best quality new strings available and tune the open strings to their proper pitches. Place your fingertip on the highest string, directly over the twelfth fret (that is, the metal fret itself). Do not press the string down—merely touch it firmly but lightly and pick the string in the usual way. This produces the string's octave harmonic. Next, *play* the note at the twelfth fret (press the string down between the eleventh and twelfth frets).

The harmonic and the fretted note should be of exactly the same pitch. If they are not, the bridge is improperly adjusted. In making this adjustment, we must assume that the harmonic is the correct pitch and the fretted note must be adjusted accordingly. If the fretted note is sharp (higher than the harmonic) the string is too short and must be lengthened by moving the bridge toward the tailpiece until the pitches are the same. If the fretted note is flat (lower than the harmonic), the string must be shortened by moving the bridge toward the neck, until the fretted and harmonic notes are identical in pitch.

If the bridge saddle is one-piece, this adjustment should be made at the first string and the last string. The center strings will be adjusted in the course of adjusting the first and last strings. Don't be concerned if, when the adjustment is complete, your bridge is at an angle. That's the usual result. In the case of bridges with individual string-length adjustment, each string should be adjusted by the same method.

Badly worn tuning machines, or strings put on improperly, will sometimes cause strings to slip out of tune. Below is a diagram illustrating the proper method for putting on strings.

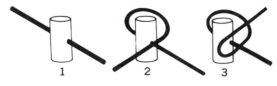

PUTTING ON STRINGS

If your machines are in good condition and your strings are put on properly, and the guitar still slips out of tune often, a vibrato tailpiece of some sort is probably to blame.

Seldom, if ever, is a neck so badly fretted or so severely warped that poor intonation results.

AMPLIFIERS/SPEAKERS

The function of an amplifier is to increase the sound of an instrument to adequately audible level —often quite high. In order to obtain faithful sound reproduction, it's necessary to employ high quality equipment. An instrument, no matter how good it is, will sound no better than the amplifier through which it's played. Roughly, it functions as follows: The sound from the instrument enters the amplifier as a weak electronic signal. The strength of this signal is increased progressively by the various stages of the amplifying circuit until, finally, it reaches the speakers as electric power in a form suitably acceptable to them. The speaker turns this electrical energy into audible energy, or sound.

Naturally any weak link in the amplifying chain may produce something less than the desired sound. There is a significant difference between hi-fi amplifiers used for home stereo and guitar amplifiers. Each is designed with its own job in view. Guitar amps, no matter how powerful and how expensive, are purposely limited in range to the type of guitar they are designed to amplify. That gives you an idea why voice systems are so different from guitar amplifiers, and why both are not readily interchangeable.

Evaluating Amplifiers

The amplifier a guitarist uses must be a compromise between adequate power and convenient size. It must have sufficient undistorted power output —enough usable sound output—to allow the instrument to be heard when it is being played with other instruments. In most cases today, this means a lot of power. Yet the amplifier must also be portable enough to accompany the player wherever he goes. This brings us to the consideration of speaker cabinets.

Speaker Cabinet: First, the speaker cabinet must be very solid. Since the speaker is being driven hard, and produces a great amount of vibration, it must be held securely in the cabinet. If the cabinet isn't sturdy, it will soon be shaken to pieces by the intense vibration of the speaker. Cabinets that are screwed and glued together are best.

In the case of bass guitar amplifiers, the cabinet serves still another purpose. A properly designed speaker cabinet encloses the speaker almost completely. This means that the speaker, vibrating in a sealed enclosure, has its vibrations limited by the cushion of air contained in the enclosed space. As is the case with all vibrating objects, speakers producing low notes vibrate slower but move further. Therefore, a speaker used to produce low notes will soon tear itself apart because of its violent backward and forward vibration if it's not constrained by a sealed cabinet. So it's necessary that a bass amplifier have a speaker cabinet not only large enough to house its speaker but also sealed to provide the necessary air cushion.

A different situation occurs in the amplifier used with lead or rhythm guitar. Since these guitars produce notes in the middle and high ranges, their speakers are not forced to move as far, but instead are driven faster and must be free and unrestricted. Therefore, they require a sturdy, open-back cabinet.

With either bass or guitar speaker cabinets, the sound-producing efficiency is increased considerably by having the cabinet solidly contact the floor, causing the floor to vibrate and employing the room itself as an aid in producing the sound. Speaker cabinets left on dollies, or other lifts, produce noticeably poor transmission of sound—especially in the lower range.

Some speaker cabinets, besides housing the speaker, also contain the amplifying unit. In the case of the closed-back cabinet, this isn't possible, since it affords no air circulation for the transistors or tubes. That's why many amplifiers, particularly those with close-backed speakers, aren't contained in the speaker cabinet, but in separate cabinets of their own. This separate power unit also isolates the delicate tubes or transistors and their complex wiring from possible damage produced by the incessant vibration of the speaker.

Loud Speakers: Since even the best designed speakers are relatively inefficient compared to the rest of the amplifying system, it's important that the best quality speakers be used in order to take fullest possible advantage of the amplifier. It's even possible to realize a significant increase in power output by using a better speaker than is supplied with the amplifier. Single 12-inch speakers can be purchased for $4.00 to as much as $150.00.

Bass speakers are usually more heavily built than guitar speakers, and the preference seems to be toward the larger diameters—at least 12, 15 and sometimes 18 inches. Lead and rhythm guitar amplifiers generally use smaller speakers, most often 10 or 12 inch. The smaller diameter speakers reproduce highs better and respond more quickly than the larger ones. The number of speakers is not terribly important. However, multiple speakers will better accommodate high-powered amplifiers.

The amount of speaker-cone area determines the amount of volume available from the amplifier. If more sound coverage (not necessarily volume) is desired, external speakers may be employed. Most better-quality amplifiers feature one or more external speaker output jacks.

Two or more amplifiers may be used by one instrument as shown by the following diagram.

When connecting amplifiers this way, be sure to do it with the amplifiers *unplugged*—not merely switched off. Of course, two amplifiers may also be used with the stereo-wired guitar.

Channels: Most amplifiers today have two channels, although there are some single-channel and some multi-channel amplifiers. The fact that an amplifier has two or more channels, with independent sets of controls for each, doesn't mean that the amplifier is to be used by more than one instrument. Since the two channels are joined together inside the amplifier at a very early stage in the power boosting chain, all the sound is eventually amplified together and reproduced by the speakers. With two guitars the amplifier and speakers will be overloaded and distortion will result.

Transistors versus Tubes: Amplifier manufacturers are rapidly converting from tube-type amplifiers to transistor or solid-state amplifiers. However, this change has not met with the approval of all guitar players and at this writing the choice of the professionals seems to be tube amplifiers. Some of the reasons for this preference are:

    a. Transistors and tubes produce quite different sounds.

    b. Pre-amplifier transistors tend to overload and distort when used with a powerful instrument.

    c. As yet transistor replacement is not

as expedient as is tube replacement and must be made by a competent electronic serviceman although transistors don't frequently burn out.

d. The weight and space saved by using transistors is lost by heat-dissipating devices necessary with high-output transistors.

Doo-Dads

Controls: (Volume) The volume control determines the volume level at which the amplifier is to operate. The numbering system of these controls isn't significant since manufacturers often employ a control which has a sharp rise in volume from number 1 to numbers 3 or 4 and barely any increase through the remaining numbers. This gives the false illusion of tremendous power in reserve.

(Tone) Amplifiers with one tone control produce most bass with the control in the extreme counter-clockwise position and most treble in the extreme clockwise position. Some amplifiers have as many as five tone controls, labelled bass, treble, middle, presence, and bright or ultra-high. Other amplifiers may have their tone control combinations further augmented by a switch which provides a general tone-range setting. These various switch positions may be called by such names as "jazz," "high," "low," "brilliant," "mellow," and so forth.

(Tremolo) There are generally two tremolo controls—one which controls the tremolo speed or rate, and one which controls its intensity or depth. A foot switch, on a cord leading from the amplifier, turns the tremolo on or off.

(Reverberation) The reverb control allows the player to select the amount of reverb or echo that he wishes to use. It, too, may be used in conjunction with a foot switch.

Special Inputs: Occasionally an amplifier may have special purpose input jacks marked bright/ normal, instrument/microphone or accordion/ microphone/guitar/bass. Your instrument works best when plugged into the correct input although you may be pleased with different sounds you might get from mis-matched inputs.

Standby: In the case of tube amplifiers a standby switch is often provided which allows the amplifier to be kept idle, but not shut off completely when temporarily not in use. Switching a tube amplifier on and off shortens tube life and, if the amplifier is going to be used for an extended

period of time, with occasional periods of rest for the player, it's best that the amplifier be left on, or switched to standby; not turned off.

Ground: The ground switch incorporated in most better amplifiers virtually reverses the plug in the wall socket. Of the two possible ways an amplifier may be plugged into the wall, one is best. Should your amplifier produce a low annoying hum, when in operation, reversing the plug itself, or activating the ground or polarity switch on the amplifier should eliminate or minimize this line noise.

Flip the switch, too, if you get a slight shock when you touch the guitar and amplifier panel, or the guitar and any part of your sound system.

Fuses: If a major disturbance or malfunction occurs in an amplifier, the resulting damage is kept to a minimum by the amplifier's safety valve —the fuse. When the fuse blows, the amplifier becomes totally inoperative. Even the pilot light goes out. If you look at the fuse you can probably tell the cause of the problem. Overloading or old fuses simply break in the center of the lead. Replace with a new fuse of equal rating and everything will be all right.

'Shorts' cause the lead to splatter inside the glass fuse. Replacing the fuse won't help. Manufacturers claim that 90% of blown fuses are a result of faulty tubes. Usually the power tubes go first. They are the large glass tubes that get the hottest and take the abuse. Jarring causes damage. They frequently come in pairs. In the event of trouble, replace one or both of those with a spare. Have them tested when you can. If however, your amplifier continually blows its fuse, it's an indication of serious disorder within the amplifier. By no means should you try to bypass the fuse or replace it with a fuse of higher amperage.

Selecting An Amplifier

The selection of an amplifier should be made carefully and with the following factors in mind: quality of sound, power (somewhat more than adequate for your needs), size and weight (i.e. portability), durability, the amplifier's reputation among the best players, appropriateness of purpose (closed back for basses, open back for guitars), desired features (such as reverberation, etc.), price (in most cases there are no amplifier "bargains"). Beware of used amplifiers.

Your guitar is only as good as its amplifier so for best results, remember—no more than one instrument for each amplifier!